New York:

STATE CENSUS OF ALBANY COUNTY TOWNS IN 1790

Compiled by

KENNETH SCOTT

CLEARFIELD

Reprinted for
Clearfield Company, Inc. by
Genealogical Publishing Co., Inc.
Baltimore, Maryland
1991, 2003

Library of Congress Catalogue Card Number 75-7592
International Standard Book Number: 0-8063-0637-4

Made in the United States of America

FOREWORD

Resolve V in the New York State constitution of April, 1777, stipulated that seven years after the termination of the war then in progress there should be taken, under the direction of the legislature, a census of the electors and inhabitants in the state. In the New York State Library is a package labelled, in the handwriting of the distinguished archivist Arnold J. F. Van Laer, "Rensselaerswyck Mss, State Census 1790. Heads of Families in various towns in Albany County. Names vary in some cases from those given in the Federal Census of the same year."

The census records in this package were badly burned in the disastrous fire in the State Library in March, 1911, and the package remained unopened until the fall of 1974, when the paper was treated to permit handling. The pages have been reproduced and copies are now available for study in the State Library and in The New-York Historical Society.

The towns covered in the State Census of Albany County are Albany (the three wards), Cambridge, Catskill, Coxsackie, Duanesburgh, Freehold, Halfmoon, Hoosick, Schenectady, Schoharie, Stephentown, Stillwater and Watervliet. About half of the names were wholly or partially destroyed in the fire, but there remain just under four thousand names. Hundreds of these vary from the listing in the Federal Census of the same year, so the importance of the State Census emerges at once. As examples of variants may be cited the following: Tys De Lamp (state) and Titus De Camp (fed.); Gonsale (state) and Kumsales (fed.); Dutcher (state) and Decker (fed.); Buys (state) and Berys (fed.).

This publication (now made possible by kind permission of the New York State Library and the New-York Historical Society) gives, first, the name as it appears in the State Census and, immediately after it, in brackets, the reading in the Federal Census. The names in the State Census are here listed alphabetically within each town, or within each ward in the City of Albany. In many instances the names in the State Census follow the same order as in the Federal Census, but the sequence is by no means identical. Sometimes, in Albany for example, the names correspond quite closely, but in other towns there are wide differences.

The State Census has the seven following headings: 1. Names of the Heads of Families; 2. Number of Male inhabitants possessed of Freeholds in the State to the Value of £100; 3. Number of Male Inhabitants possessed of Freeholds in the County to the Value of £20; 4. Number of Male Inhabitants Renting tenements to the Value of 40s. who have paid Taxes; 5. males; 6. females; 7. slaves. The destruction of these statistics was so extensive that their reproduction here would present an enormous problem. It is suggested, therefore, that if a name is located a check may be made under that name in the photographic reproductions in one of the two libraries that have them.

ALBANY - First Ward
Allen, ... (Allen, Solomon)
Allen, ... (Allen, William)
Andrews, ...
Arnold, ... (Arnold, Eli)
Ashmore, ... (Ashmore, John)
Askins, ... (Askins, Benjamin)
Babcock, (Jo)shua, (Babcock, Joshua)
Baldwin, ... (Baldwin, William)
Barrett, ... (Barrett, Peter)
Barrett, ... (Barritt, Thomas)
Barry, ... (Barry, Thomas)
Barskins, ... (Baskins, Elizabeth)
Bennet, ... (Bennet, Owen)
Blake, (Ja)mes (Blake, James)
Bloodgood, ... (Bloodgood, Abraham)
Bloomendall, ... (Bloomindall, Jacob)
Bloomendal, ... (Bloomendall, Maus)
Bloore, ... (Bloore, Joshua)
Bogert, ... (Bogert, Henry)
Bostwick, Anne (Bostwick, Anne)
Brass, ... (Brass, John)
Bratt, ... (Bradt, Henry B.)
Brown, (M)artina (Brown, Martina)
Campbell, Alexander (Campbell, Alexander)
Campbell, ... (Campbell, Archibald)
Campston, ... (Cumpston, Edward)
Capron, Wi(lliam) (Capron, William)
Carlo, ... (Carlo, Stephen)
Chambers, (Fr)ances (Chambers, Frances)
Clark, Patrick (Clark, Patrick)
Clement, ... (Clement, Jane)
Collins, ... (Collins, William)
Cooper, ... (Cooper, Obediah)
Cozzens, ... (Cozzins, Isachar)
Crane, ...
Cugler, (Matt)hew (Cugler, Matthew)
Dawson, ... (Dawson, Volkert)
De Garmo, (Ra)chel (De Garmo, Rachel)
Dennis, Daniel (Dennis, Daniel)
Denniston, Isaac (Denniston, Isaac)
Dewitt, ... (De Wite, Simeon)
Dole, (Ja)mes (Dole, James)
Dourye, ... (Drurye, Nicholas)
Dunneway, ... (Dunneway, James)
Eggleston, ... (Eggleston, John)
Fair(lie), ... (Fairlie, James)
Fife, ... (Fife, Isabel)
Fryer, ... (Fryer, John)
(Ge)rritson, ... (Gerritson, Frederick)
Gibson, ... (Gibson, Colin)
Gibson, ... (Gibson, David)
Goewy, ... (Gowey, Garret)
Gordon, Charles (Gordon, Charles)

Grant, G[eorge] [Grant, George]
Grant, ... [Grant, John]
Gray, ... [Gray, Robert]
Guyer, ... G. [Guyer, John G.]
Hallenbake, ... [Halenbeck, Barnardus]
Hallenbeck, ... [Halenbeck, James]
Henry, ... [Henry, Cuffee]
Hewson, Anne [Hewson, Ann]
Heyer, ... [Heyer, Garrit]
Hilton, ...
Hilton, ... [Hilton, John]
Hilton, ... [Hilton, Peter W.]
Hilton, ... [Hilton, Thomas]
Hilton, William B. [Hilton, William B.]
Hogen, ... [Hogen, Henry]
Hoogkerk, ... [Hoogkerk, Abraham]
Hoogkerk, ... [Hoogkirk, Isaac]
Hun, Hamen [Hunn, Harmen]
Hun, [Ma]rgaret [Hunn, Margaret]
Hun, ... [Hunn, Thomas D.]
Johnson, [Jerem]iah [Johnson, Jeremiah]
Joice, ... [Joyce, George]
Jolly, ... [Jolly, James]
Kelly, ... [Kelley, Thomas]
Kirkland, [Will]iam [Kirkland, William]
Klinck, George
Lansing, ...ie [Lansing, Ariantic]
Lansing, [Tho]mas [Lansing, Thomas]
Lansingh, ... [Lansing, Peter]
Ledius, Bal[tus] [Ledius, Baltus]
Lewis, ... H. [Lewis, Samuel H.]
Lundegreen, ... F. [Flundegron, Charles F.]
[Mc]Clalie[?], ... [Mc Clallen, Robert]
[Mc G]lachan, ... [Mc Glachen, Rachel]
Mc Glashon, Charles [Mc Glashon, Charles]
Mc Gourk, ...
Mc Hargh, ... [Mc Hargh, John]
Mc Pherson, Duncan [Mc Pherson, Duncan]
Mahar, ... [Mahar, William]
Marrough, ... [Marrough, James]
Martin, [J]anet [Martin, Janet]
Menzie, [Jo]hn [Menzie, John]
Merselius, ... [Marselus, Henry]
Miller, ... [Miller, Margarit]
Mitchell, ... [Mitchell, Thomas]
Molat, [Susa]nnah [Molat, Susannah]
Montieth, [P]atrick [Montieth, Patrick]
Morgan, ... [Morgan, Charles]
Murphy, ... [Murphy, John]
Mynderse, [Abr]aham [Mynderse, Abraham]
Mynderse, Martin [Mynderse, Martin]
Nellinger, ... [Nellinger, Joseph]
Ostrander, ... [Ostrander, John]
Paget, ... [Paget, John]

```
Price, ... (Price, John)
Pruyn, John J. (Pruyn, John J.)
Radlie, ... (Radlie, Martia)
Radly, ... (Raddley, Jacobus)
Radly, ... (Raddley, John L.)
Redley, ... (Radley, Henry)
Reollie (?)
Robison, ... (Robison, John)
Ross, ... (Ross, James)
Rutherford, ... (Rutherfurd, Archibald)
Ryckman, (Ga)rrit (Ryckman, Garret)
Ryckman, ... (Rickmann, Peter)
Schuyler, ... (Schuyler, Philip)
Scott, ... (Scott, John)
Shell, ...
(Sh)ipboy, ... (Shipboy, Thomas)
Spencer, ... (Spencer, Thomas)
Spiers, ... (Spiers, John)
Stewart, ... (Stewart, John)
Tayler, ... (Tayler, John)
Taylor, John (Taylor, John, shoemaker)
Thompson, ... (Thompson, Ralph)
Tolman, ... (Tolman, Joseph)
Trotter, (Matth)ew (Trotter, Matthew)
Truax, ... (Truax, Jacob)
Van Ale(n), ... (Van Allen, John)
Van Benthuysen, ...
Van Benthuysen, ... (Van Benthuysen, Baltus)
Van Benthuysen, ... (Van Benthuysen, William)
Van Bergen, P(eter) (Van Bergen, Peter)
(Van Du)sen, ... (Van Dusen, Peter)
(Va)n Ingen, ... (Vn Ingen, William)
Van Rensselaer, Philip S. (Van Rensselaer, Philip
                                               S.)
Van Sante, ... (Van Zant, Elanor)
Van Sant, ... us (Van Zant, Jacobus)
Van Scaick, ... (Van Schaick, Stephen)
Van Veghten, ... (Van Vechten, Ephraim)
Van Veghten, ... (Van Vechten, Jane)
Van Waggoner, ... (Van Waggoner, Henry)
Van Waggoner, (P)hilip (Van Waggoner, Philip)
(Van) Wie, ... (Van Wee, William)
Veeder, ... (Veeder, Volkert S.)
Vossburgh, ...
Wans, ...
Webster, Charles R. (Webster, Charles R.)
Wendell, ... (Wendell, Hendrick)
Wendell, ... W. (Wendell, John W.)
(We)ndell, ... (Wendell, Philip)
Wilkinson, ... (Wilkinson, John)
Willis, ... (Willis, Rachel)
Winkworth, ... (Winkworth, John)
Wood, ...
Wyngart, ...
```

Yates, ... (Yates, Albertus)
Yates, ... I. (Yates, Abraham I.)
Young, ... (Young, John)

ALBANY - Second Ward
Andrews, ... (Andrews, Joseph)
Archer, ... (Archer, George)
Barrington, Lewes (Barrington, Lewis)
Bleeker, Catelynta (Bleeker, Catelintia)
Bleeker, Jno N. (Bleeker, John N.)
Bogart, Abr^m (Bogert, Abraham)
Boyd, Jno (Boyd, John)
Brewer, Jno (Brower, John)
Bromny, Saml (Bromley, Samuel)
Brower, Corn^s (Brower, Cornelius)
Bruce, Robt (Bruce, Robert)
Cammeron, Jno (Cammeron, John)
Campbell, Jno (Campbell, John)
Carson, Alex^r (Carson, Alexander)
Carson, Jno (Carson, John)
Christie, ... (Christie, John)
Cuyler, Abrah^m (Cuyler, Abraham)
Dale, Wm. (Dale, William)
Davis, Peter (Davis, Peter)
Douglas, Thom^s (Douglass, Thomas)
Fadon, ... (Fadon, John)
Finch, Isaac (Finch, Isaac)
Fuller, James (Fuller, James)
Giles, Willm (Giles, William)
Groesbeck, Corn^s (Groesbeck, Cornelius)
Haines, Thomas (Haynes, Thomas)
Hannah, ... (Hannah, Samuel)
Hanson, Albert (Hanson, Albert)
Hay, Alex^r (Hay, Alexander)
Heath, Jno (Heath, John)
Horse, George (Horse, George)
James, John (James, John)
Katling, Gerr^t (Keating, Garret)
Kennear, Jam^s (Kennear, James)
Lyn, Aaron (Lyn, Aaron)
Mc Dermot, Mich^l (Mc Durmot, Michael)
Mc Donald, Donald (Mc Donald, Donald)
Mc Gurgy, Edwd (Mc Gurgy, Edward)
Mc Kenney, Jno (Mc Kenney, John)
Mc Manac, W^m (Mc Manac, William)
Mc Mickle, ... (Mc Mickle, John)
Magee, Jno (Magee, John)
Merchant, ... (Merchant, George)
Miggs, Seth (Meggs, Seth)
Mucalroy, Jno (not in Fed. Census)
Mulligan, Jam^s (Milligan, James)
Myer, Carol (Myer, Carol)
Park, Henry (Park, Henry)
Pouyn, ... F. (Pruyn, John F.)

Quitman, Jno (not in Fed. Census)
Rider, Bart (Rider, Barent)
Ruby, Conradt (Ruby, Conradt)
Ryan, Patrick (Ryan, Patrick)
Shancklin, Andrw (not in Fed. Census)
Snyder, Danl (Snyder, Daniel)
Staats, Bart G. (Staats, Barent G.)
Staats, Henry (Staats, Henry)
Sturges, Isaac (Sturges, Isaac)
Ten Eyck, Marms (Ten Eyck, Harmanus)
Tiffany, Sylvester (Tiffany, Silvester)
Vn Ness, ... (Van Ness, John)
Van Rensselaer, Jerh (Vn Rensselaer, Jeremiah)
Vn Schurlyne, Corns (Vn Schurlyne, Cornelius)
Vn Vranken, Maus R. (Van Vrankin, Moses R.)
Vn Zant, Jno W. (Van Zant, John W.)
Vissher, ... (Vissher, Matthew)
Waggoner, Andw (Waggoner, Andrew)
Whipple, Benjn (Whipple, Benjamin)
Willett, Edwd, Jun. (Willitt, Edward, Junr)
Wilmott, Jno (Wilmot, John)
Winne, Jacob (Winne, Jacob)
Winne, Killean D. (Winne, Killian D.)

ALBANY - Third Ward
Beekman, Christopher (Beekman, Christopher)
Beekman, Widow Elizabeth (Beekman, Elizabeth)
Bleecker, ... (Bleeker, Barent)
Bloodgood, James (Bloodgood, James)
Bower, Barent (Bower, Barent)
Boyd, John (Boyd, John)
Bratt, Henry (Bradt, Henry)
Bratt, Teunis (Bradt, Teunis)
Caldwell, James (Caldwell, James)
Dean, Stewart (Dean, Stewart)
Douw, Catherine (Douw, Catherine)
Dunbar, William (Dunbar, William)
Eights, Abraham (Eights, Abraham)
Fonda, David (Fonda, David)
Gansevoort, Harme (Gansevoort, Harman)
Gansevoort, ..., Junr (Gansevoort, Leonard, Junr)
Gates, John (Gates, John)
Glen, Cornelius (Glen, Cornelius)
Graham, Theodorus Van W (Graham, Theodorus Van
                                            Wyck)
Graveraet, Henry (Graverato, Henry)
Groesbeeck, Gerrit (Groesbeck, Garrit)
Hale, Daniel (Hale, Daniel)
Hun, Thomas (Hunn, Thomas)
Hun, William (Hunn, William)
Izebrass, Widow (Icebrass, Hannah)
Jauncey, John (Jauncey, John)
Kirk, John (Kirk, John)
Lansing, Gerrit, Junr (Lansing, Garrit, Junr)

Lansing, Gerrit A. (Lansing, Gerrit A.)
Lansing, Jacob G. (Lansing, Jacob G.)
Leonard, ... (Leonard, Enock)
Lewis, ... (Lewis, Samuel)
McCready, William (McReady, William)
(M^c)Millan, ... (McMillen, John)
Maley, John (Maley, John)
Melton, Henry (Milton, Henry)
Miller, Philip, Junr (Miller, Philip, Junr)
Orr, Widow Isabel (Orr, Isabel)
Pruyn, Widow Neltie (Pruyn, Nailsha)
Robeseau, James (Robisan, James)
Roff, John (Roff, John)
Roseboom, Dirck (Roseboom, Dirick)
Roseboom, Widow Eve (Roseboom, Eve)
Sim, Peter (Sim, Peter)
Slingerlandt, Jacob (Slingerland, Jacob)
Smith, Widow Ann (Smith, Ann)
Stansil, Daniel (Stansil, Daniel)
Ten Broeck, Abraham (Ten Broeck, Abraham)
Van Antwerp, Daniel (Van Antwerp, Daniel)
Van Denbergh, Gerrit (Vanderburg, Garrit)
Van Derheyden, Jacob (Vander Heyden, Jacob)
Van Iveren, Rynier M. (Van Iveren, Rynier)
Van Vranken, Gerrit (Van Vronkin, Garrit)
Veeder, John (Veeder, John)
Visscher, Gerrit T. (Visscher, Garrit T.)
Waters, David (Waters, David)
Willett, Elbert (Willett, Elbert)
Williamson, James (Williamson, James)
Williamson, Timothy (Williamson, Timothy)
Wynans, Stephen (Wynants, Stephen)
Wynkoop, ... (Wynkoop, Jacobus)

CAMBRIDGE
Bell, ... (Bell, Isaac)
Bell, ... (Bell, Josiah)
Bell, ... (Bell, Phineas)
(Ca)ldwell, ... (Caldwell, Joseph)
Cook, Benjn (Cook, Benjn)
Dewell, Benjn (Duel, Benjn)
Dewell, Corn^s (Duel, Cornelius)
Dewell, Gideon (Duel, Gideon)
Hodge, ... (Hodge, Israel)
Hodge, ... (Hodge, Solomon)
McClannen, ... (McClellen, John)
(Pu)tman, ... (Putman, Abijah)
Rawley, Walter (Rawley, Walter)
Shelly, John (Shelly, John)
Shelly, W^m (Shelly, Willm)
(S)houlder, ... (Shoulder, Andrew)
Wells, Edmond (Wells, Edmond)
Wells, Shaler (Wells, Shaylor)
Wing, ... (Wing, John)

Wyer, ... (Wier, John)

CATSKILL
Abel, Garret (Abeel, Garret)
Abell, David (Abeel, David)
Adams, ... (Adams, Joseph)
Adams, ... (Adams, Josiah)
Allen, ... (Allen, Samuel)
Anally, William (Anniley, William)
Beach, ... (Beach, Ebenezer)
Beach, ... (Beach, Noah)
Becker, Jacob (Becker, Jacob)
Berger, Coenrat (Bergen, Conradt)
Blaw, ... (Blann, Uriah)
Bogardus, ... (Bogardus, Abraham)
Bogardus, ... (Bogardus, Egbert)
Bogardus, ... (Bogardus, James)
Bogardus, ... (Bogardus, Peter)
(Bos)tick, ... (Bostwick, John)
Brando, John (Brandon, John)
Brando, William, Junr (Brandon, William, Junr)
Brandow, ... (Brandon, Hieronimus)
Britt, Peter (Britt, Peter)
Brockway, Gideon (Brockway, Gideon)
Brown, James (Brown, James)
B...unham, ... (Brusnaham, Andrew)
Bush, David (Bush, David)
Camp, (Elis)ha (Camp, Elisha)
Campbell, John (Campbell, John)
Cargel, James (Cargel, James)
Cash, Silvenus (Cash, Silvenus)
Caulder, James (Colder, James)
(Ch)arlotte, ... (Charlotte, William)
(C)hase, ... (Chase, Isaac)
Chase, Thomas (Chase, Thomas)
Claw, Evert (Claw, Evert)
(Cle)mens, ... (Clement, Patrick)
Coddington, Joseph (Coddington, Joseph)
Coller, ... (Coller, Oliver)
Dailey, ... (Dailey, John)
(Ded)rick, ... (Dedrick, Zachariah)
Degroot,....., (Groot, Cornelius D.)
(De)milt, ... (Mite, Anthony)
Dickeson, Hezekiah (Dickinson, Hezekiah)
Dies, John (Dies, John)
Drake, Joseph (Drake, Joseph)
Drumond, Robert (Drummond, Robert)
(Du)bois, ... (Dubois, Barent)
Dubois, Isaac (Dubois, Isaac)
Dumond, David (Dumond, David)
Dumond, John B. (Dumond, John B.)
Dumond, William (Dumond, William)
(Dun)ham, ... (Dunham, Samuel)
Ecker, Jacob (Ecker, Jacob)

Egbertse, Barent (Egbertse, Barent)
Egbertse, Cornelius (Egbertse, Cornelius)
Egbertse, ... (Egbertse, John)
Ewman, Andrew (Aman, Andrew)
(Fl)aake, ... (Flaake, ...nah)
Freligh, ... (Freligh, John)
Fretshorn, Isaac (Tushorn, Isaac)
Gersie, Joseph (Gersie, Joseph)
Goetsious, Jacob (Gatchins, Jacob)
Gordon, ... (Gordon, John)
Grims, ... (Grymes, Richard)
Haight, ... (Haight, Samuel)
Hallenbeck, ... (Hallenbeck, Jacob)
(Hal)lenbeck, ... (Hallenbeck, Samuel)
Hallenbeeck, Jacob (Hallenbeck, Jacob)
Hallenbeeck, ... (Hallenbeck, John)
Hallenbeeck, John C. (Hallenbeck, Jacob C.)
Hendrickse, ... (Hendricksen, Hendrick)
Hendrickse, Matthew (Hendrickson, Matthew)
(Herma)nse, ... (Hermanse, Gosin)
Hons, ... (House, John)
Hotlin, ... (Hotlin, Isaac)
(J)ackson, ... (Jackson, Daniel)
Jurry, ... Holden (Gury, Samuel Holden)
Keeler, ... (Keeler, Ezra)
Kidney, ...
Kidney, ... (Kidney, Roeliff)
Knoll, ... (Knoll, Henry)
Lamb, ... (Lamb, Able)
Leeman, Clement, Junr (Leeming, Clement, Junr)
Leeman, Jacob (Leeman, Jacob)
Leeman, Jacob, Junr (Leeming, Jacob, Junr)
Leeman, Jeremiah (Leeming, Jeremiah)
Leeman, John (Leeming, John)
Leurs, Joseph (Lewis, Joseph)
Losier, Oliver (Leshier, Oliver)
McDarmit, ... (McDurmot, Francis)
McFall, Niel (McFall, Neal)
Martin, Frederick (Martin, Frederick)
Mellery, John (Millery, John)
Meyer, Christian (Myer, Christian)
Milkhouse, Coenraet (Milkhouse, Conradt)
Miller, Joseph (Miller, Joseph)
Milligan, ... (Milligan, James)
Morrison, ... (Morrison, James)
Morrison, ... (Morrison, John)
Mosher, Jacob (Moushour, Jacob)
Mosher, ... (Monsher, Thomas)
Mowers, Peter (Mowers, Peter)
Munden, John (Mundin, John)
Newkerk, Gerardus (Newkirk, Gerardus)
Newkerk, Jacob (Newkirk, Jacob)
Nicholas, ... (Nichols, Eli)
Oajo, Charles (Cudjo, Charles)

O Brien, Jeremiah (O'Brien, Jeremiah)
Oothoudt, Henry (Oothoudt, Henry)
Overpagh, Peter J. (Cverpagh, Peter I.)
Overpagh, Wilhelmus (Overpagh, Wilhelmus)
Owens, ... (Owens, John)
Palmer, ... (Palmer, Stephen)
Park, Thomas (Park, Thomas)
Persen, Henry (Person, Henry)
Persen, James (Person, James)
Person, John (Pierson, John)
Person, John, Junr (Pierson, John, Junr)
Post, Samuel (Post, Samuel)
Rightmyer, ... (Rightmyer, Johannes)
(Right)myer, ... (Rightmyer, William)
Rodgers, ... (Rogers, Zepheniah)
(R)ows, ... (Rows, John)
Rushmore, ... (Rushmore, Jeremiah)
Rushmore, Samuel (Rushmore, Samuel)
Rushmore, Silas (Rushmore, Silas)
Salsbury, Abraham (Salisbury, Abraham)
Salsbury, ... (Salisbury, Barent S.)
Salsbury, Frances (Salisbury, Francis)
Sands, ... (Sands, Henry)
Sax, John (Socks, John)
Schanemon, John^s (Schaneman, John)
Schomaker, ... (Schonmaker, Michael)
Schram, Clement (Schrem, Clement)
Schram, ... (Schrem, Clement)
Schram, Frederick (Schrem, Frederick)
Schut, ... (Schut, Peter)
Schut, Solomon (Schut, Solomon)
Schut, Solomon (Schut, Solomon)
(S)ell, ... (Sill, Shaderick)
Shipmouse, ... (Schapmouse, John)
Slanter, ... (Slauter, Amos)
Smith, Frederick (Smith, Frederick)
Smith, ... (Smith, Michael)
Smith, ... (Smith, Peter)
Souser, ... (Souser, Johannes)
Souser, Peter (Souser, Peter)
Steenbergh, (Jeremi)ah (Steenbergh, Jeremiah)
Steenbergh, ... (Steenbergh, John)
Symons, ... (Symons, Robert)
Ten Broeck, Gerritie (Ten Brock, Garrittie)
Thompson, John (Thompson, John)
Tibbets, Henry (Tibbets, Henry)
Timmerman, ... (Timmerman, Margaret)
Titus, ... (Titus, Nathaniel)
Trompour, Nicholas (Trumphour, Nicholas)
Van Begen, William (Van Bergen, William)
Van Bergen, David (Van Bergen, David)
Van Bergen, Martin (Van Bergen, Martin)
Van Dyck, Wessel (Van Dyke, Wessel)
Van Etten, John (Van Etten, John)

Van Etten, Peter (Van Etten, Peter)
Van Garde, Abraham (Van Garde, Abraham)
Van Garde, Peter (Van Garde, Peter)
(Van G)elden, ... (Van Gelden, Peter)
Van Hoesen, ... (Van Husin, Casper)
Van Hoesen, Gerrit (Van Husin, Garrit)
Van Hoesen, Jacob J. (Van Husin, Jacob J.)
(Va)n Loon, ... (Van Loon, Albertus)
(Van) Loon, ... (Van Loon, John M.)
Van Loon, Peter (Van Loon, Peter)
Van Orden, ... (Van Orden, Egnatius)
Van Orden, ... (Van Orden, Hezekiah)
Van Orden, ... (Van Orden, John)
Van Schaick, Gosen (Van Schaick, Gosin)
Van Schaick, Sybrant (Van Schaick, Sybrant)
Van Valkenburgh, Isaac (Van Volkenbergh, Isaac)
Van Valkenburgh, Lambert (Van Volkenburg, Lambert)
Van Veghten, ... (Van Vechtin, Jacob)
(Va)n Veghten, ... (Van Vechten, Samuel)
Van Veghten, Teunis D. (Van Vechten, Teunis D.)
Vedder, Catherine (Veeder, Catherine)
Wall, Frederick (Wall, Frederick)
Wells, ... (Wills, Philip)
Wells, ... (Wills, William)
Whiley, Alexander (Whiley, Alexander)
Whiting, Thomas (Whiting, Thomas)
Wiswal, ... (Wiswell, Amasa)
Witbeeck, (A)nnaka (Witbeck, Annaka)
(W)olf, ... (Wolf, Jeremiah)
Wynkoop, Peter (Wynkoop, Peter)
Young, James (Young, James)

COXSACKIE
(Ad)ams, ... (Adams, Peter C.)
Allin, ... (Allen, Noah)
Anderson, John (Anderson, John)
Annbell, David (Annebell, David)
Austin, Widow Elizebet (Austin, Elizabeth)
Balding, Andrew (Baldwin, Andrew)
Barker, ... (Barker, Richard)
(Bar)tholomew, ... (Bartholomew, Pheneas)
Begordus, Jacob (Bogardus, Jacob)
Belles, Jabez (Bellows, Jabez)
Benton, Isaac (Benton, Isaac)
Berton, ... (Barton, William)
Blackmore, Titus (Blackmore, Titus)
Blacksly, Isaac (Blakesley, Isaac)
Blaksly, Samuel (Blakeley, Samuel)
Bogardus, Ephriam, Junr (Bogardus, Ephraim, Junr)
Boom, John (Boom, John)
Boom, Mathias (Boom, Matthias)
Bostwick, David
Bothe, Luther (Booth, Luther)
Botsford, David (Botsford, David)

Brandaw, Peter (Brando, Peter)
Brewster, David (Brewster, David)
Bronk, Caspares (Bronk, Casparus)
Bronk, Ephriam (Bronk, Ephraim)
Bronk, Peter (Bronk, Peter)
Bronk, Philip (Bronk, Philip)
Brownel, ... (Brundell, Nathaniel)
Bulk, ... (Bulk, Reuben)
Burraughs, Nathan (Burroughs, Nathan)
Butts, ...ham (Butts, Gershom)
Butts, (Ric)hard (Butts, Richard)
(Ca)nine, (Philip), Junr (Canine, Philip, Junr)
Canniff, Abraham (Canif, Abraham)
Canniff, Jeremiah (Canif, Jeremiah)
Chichester, ... (Chichester, Sophia)
Chikester, James (Chychester, James)
Clauw, Frans (Clow, Francis)
Clauw, ... (Clow, Jeremiah)
Claw, ... C. (Clow, John C.)
Cole, Jacob L. (Cole, Jacob L.)
Collins, Edward (Collins, Edward)
Colyer, Dirick (Collier, Direck)
Colyer, Isaac (Collier, Isaac)
Colyer, Jochem (Collier, Jochum)
Colyer, John (Collier, John)
Colyer, Teunis (Collier, Teunis)
Conine, Cornelius (Canine, Cornelius)
Cook, John (Cook, John)
Cornwell, Thomas (Cornwell, Thomas)
Crosman, Thomas (Crossman, Thomas)
Dadge, Rufus (Dodge, Rufus)
Daggot, Mahu (Daggart, Mayhew)
Davis, Jonathan (David, Jonathan)
Deyo, Christopher (De Yo, Christopher)
Dickinson, ... (Dickinson, Zebediah)
Drack, William (Drake, William)
Dudley, George (Dudley, George)
Eastman, Charles (Eastman, Charles)
Edget, Henry (Edget, Henry)
Edwards, ... (Edwards, William)
Elles, Daniel (Ellis, Daniel)
Elsworth, Arther (Elsworth, Arthur)
Essex, Benjamin (Essex, Benjamin)
Ferris, Gilbert (not in Fed. Census)
Finch, Amos (Finch, Amos)
Freligh, Benjamin (Frelegh, Benjamin)
Gage, Remmembrance (Gage, Remembrance)
Gay, Thomas (Gay, Thomas)
Gerret, John (Garret, John)
Gidney, ...
Gold, Asa (Gold, Asa)
Gold, Bennony (Gold, Benonah)
Graat, John (Groot, John)
Green, ... (Green, Isaiah)

Griffen, ... (Griffin, Gershom)
Halenbeek, Abraham (Hollenbeck, Abraham)
Hall, Aaron (Hall, Aaron)
Hallenbeek, Casper (Hallenbeck, Casper)
Hallenbeek, Casper W. (Hallenbeck, Casper W.)
Hallenbeek, Isaac (Hallenbeck, Isaac)
Halenbeek, Jocham (Hallenbeck, Jochum)
Hallenbeek, ...chum (Hallebeck, Jochum)
Hallenbeek, John (Hallenbeck, John)
Hallenbeek, Martain (Hallenbeck, Martin)
Hallenbeek, Naning (Hallenbeck, Naning)
Hallenbeek, William (Hallenbeck, William)
Hermence, ... (Hermanee, Andress N.)
Herrington, Isaac (Herrington, Isaac)
Herrington, Zackiah (Herrington, Zachariah)
Hill, Elisha (Hill, Elisha)
Hine, Lewas (Hine, Lewis)
Hitchcook, Eliab (Hitcock, Eliab)
Hoghtaling, Andrew (Houghtalen, Andrew)
Hoghtaling, Conraat (Houghtalen, Conradt)
Hoghtaling, Conradt (Houghtalen, Conradt F.)
Hoghtaling, Henry C. (Houghtalen, Henry C.)
Hoghtaling, Thomas (Houghtalen, Thomas)
Hollenbeek, ...M. (Hallenbeck, Casper M.)
(Holl)enbeek, ... (Hollenbeck, Jacob)
Holmes, (Je)dediah (Holmes, Jedediah)
Holms, Benjamin (Holmes, Benjamin)
Homan, ... (Homan, John)
Horton, Peleg (Horton, Peleg)
Hudson, Asa (Hudson, Asa)
(Hun)tington, ... (Huntington, Reuben)
Husted, John (Husted, John)
Jackson, Jacob (Jackson, Jacob)
Jansen, Patrus (Yanser, Petrus)
Jared, William (Gerard, William)
Jones, Peter (Jones, Peter)
King, Obediah (King, Obediah)
Kinyou, Griffen (Kennion, Griffin)
Ladue, Peter (La duc, Peter)
Lake, Mathew (Lake, Matthew)
Lake, Thomas (Lake, Thomas)
Lake, Timothy (Lake, Timothy)
Lane, ... (Lane, Gilbert)
(Lanf)ier, ... (Lanfier, Henry)
Lanphman, Stephen (Lanthman, Stephen)
Lantman, Peter (Lantman, Peter)
Ledew, Abraham (Ledew, Abraham)
Ledew, Oliver (Ledew, Oliver)
Litchfield, James (Litchfield, James)
Lyns, Yanatiob (Lyons, Ignatius)
Mansfield, William (Mansfield, William)
Masters, Stephen (Masters, Stephen)
Masters, William (Masters, William)
Merlcolm, ... (Mercolm, Henry)

Michel, Elijah (Mitchell, Abijah)
Minton, Benjamin (Minthorne, Benjamin)
Morehouse, ... (Morehouse, George)
Morehouse, ... (Morehouse, Peter)
Mune, ... (Moor, Joseph)
Murray, Philow (Murray, Philo)
Nicklas, Silas (Nicholas, Silas)
North, ...emas (Norht, Orsemus)
Nucomb, Obediah (Newcome, Obediah)
Odere, Peter (Odear, Peter)
Overpage, Isaac (Overpaugh, Isaac)
Owens, Eliflet (Owens, Eliphilet)
Palmer, Elias (Palmer, Elias)
Palmer, Jonathan (Palmer, Jonathan)
Palmer, Nathaniel (Palmer, Nathaniel)
Palmer, Oliver (Palmer, Oliver)
Palmer, Robert (Palmer, Robert)
Palmer, ... (Palmer, Solomon)
Pane, Robert (Payne, Robert)
Parket, Hedeist (Parker, Thadeus)
Parkes, David (Parks, David)
Parks, Samuel (Parks, Samuel)
Patterson, ... (Patterson, Robert)
Perrey, (Ic)habod (Perry, Ichabod)
Phelps, Josiah (Phelps, Josiah)
Pickit, Ebenezer (not in Fed. Census)
Pickit, Eldert (Picket, Eldert)
Plum, ... (Plum, John)
Post, Enock (Post, Enock)
Powell, ... (Powell, Elisha)
Preston, John (Preston, John)
Provoost, ... (Provost, Abraham)
Purdy, Joseph (Purdy, Joseph)
Quimbee, Stephen (Quimby, Stephen)
Randel, Abraham (Rundel, Abraham)
Randel, Rufus (Randall, Rufus)
Randle, Reuben (Rundle, Reuben)
Reed, Abraham (Ried, Abraham)
Reed, Isaac (Reed, Isaac)
Richmon, Silvester (Richmond, Silvester)
Roberts, Ezekiel (Roberts, Ezekiel)
Robins, John (Robins, John)
Root, Adonijah (Root, Adenijah)
Root, Adonijah, Junr (Root, Adenijah, Junr)
Roots, ...hn (Roots, John)
Rosa, Hendrick (Rosa, Hendrick)
Rosa, Storm (Rose, Storm)
Rose, Geart (Rose, Garret)
Rushmore, (T)homas (Rushmore, Thomas)
Rywe, Roulof (Ryne, Roclif)
Salisburgh, Wessel (Salisbury, Wessel)
Sanford, ... (Sanfort, Aaron)
Schermerhorn, John (Schermerhorn, John)
Schram, Isaac (Schrem, Isaac)

Schram, Peter (Schrem, Peter)
(Sc)hram, ... (Schrem, William)
Seecorn, David (Secord, David)
Sellert, ... (Sellert, Peter)
Severse, Nicholas (Everse, Nicholas)
Shaddad, Peter (Sheddon, Peter)
Sharp, Jacob (Sharp, Jacob)
Shephard, Joseph (Shipperd, Joseph)
Shephard, Rufus (Shepperd, Rufus)
Signer, Albertus (Signier, Albertus)
Simons, Elijah (Simmons, Elijah)
Simons, James (Simons, James)
Smith, Christopher (Smith, Christopher)
Soper, Henry (Sooper, Henry)
Spoor, Cornelius (Spoor, Cornelius)
Spoor, Derick (Spoor, Dirick)
Spoor, ... (Spoor, Isaac)
Spoor, (Jo)hanis J. (Spoor, Johannes)
Squair, Samuel (Squire, Samuel)
Squire, Clark (Squire, Clark)
Stawson, Jehial (Slawson, Johial)
Steen, Robert (Steen, Robert)
Steenbergh, ... (Stienbarack, Cornelius)
Stockman, William (Stockman, William)
Stone, Nathan (Stone, Nathan)
Storm, ... (Storm, John)
Story, Amos (Story, Amos)
Stovy, Benjamin (Story, Benjamin)
Stratton, David (Stratton, David)
Sutherland, Joel (Southerland, Joel)
Sutherland, Smith (Southerland, Smith)
Tarbos, ... (Tarbush, Daniel)
Taylor, Daniel (Taylor, Daniel)
Thomson, John (Thompson, John)
Thorn, ... (Thorne, Ebenezer)
Thorn, ... (Thom, Edward)
Thorn, James (Thorne, James)
Titus, ... (Titus, Charles)
Torance, Joseph (not in Fed. Census)
Totton, Samuel (Totten, Samuel)
Travers, James (Travis, James)
Trowbridge, Abel (Trowbridge, Able)
Tryon, Benjamin D. (Tryon, Benjamin)
Tryon, Jochum (Tryon, Jochum)
Tryon, Peter (Tryon, Peter)
Van, ... (Van, John)
(Van) Bergen, ... (Van Bergen, Henry)
Van Bergen, Peter A. (Van Bergen, Peter A.)
Van Boskerk, Andries (Van Buskirk, Andrew)
Van Boskerk, John (Van Buskirk, John)
Van Boskerk, Lawrence A. (Van Buskirk, Lawrence A.)
Van Buskerk, (John) L. (Van Buskirk, John L.)
...d Berck, ... (Vandenbarack, Hendrick)
...den Berck, ... (Vandenburgh, John R.)

...berck, ... (Vandenbarack, Richard)
...den Berck, ... (Vandenberg, Richard R.)
...berck, ... (Vandenbarack, Wilhelmus)
...an Bergen, ... (Vandenbergen, Anthony)
Van Der Zee, Albert (Vander Zee, Albert)
Van Der Zee, Teunis (Vander Zee, Teunis)
Van Dusen, Lucas (Van Dusen, Lucas)
V(an) Loon, Albertus, Junr (Van Loon, Albertus)
Van Lone, Albert (Van Loon, Albert)
Van Lone, Jacob J. (Van Loon, Jacob J.)
(Van) Lone, ... (Van Loon, Jacob J.)
Van Lone, Jure (Van Loon, Jeremiah)
Van Lone, Nicholas (Van Loon, Nicholas)
Van Schaick, Aarent (Van Schaick, Arent)
(Van) Schaick, ... (Van Schaick, Myndert)
V(an) Valkenburgh, James (Van Volkenburgh, James)
Van Woort, Nicholas (Van Vort, Nicholas)
Vossburgh, Philip (Vossburgh, Philip)
Walker, ... (Walker, Elijah)
Walker, ... (Walker, Israel)
Walker, ... (Walker, Israel)
Warner, Den (Warner, Daniel)
Webber, Henry (Webber, Henry)
Weeks, Henry (Weeks, Henry)
Wells, Abraham (Wells, Abraham)
Wells, ..., Junr (Wells, William, Junr)
Wheler, Ezekiel (Weeler, Ezekel)
White, Elijah (White, Elijah)
White, Fredrick (White, Frederick)
Whiten, Ichabod (Wuton, Ichabod)
William, Thomas (Williams, Thomas)
Willson, James (Wilson, James)
Willson, John (Willson, John)
Witbeek, Isaac (Witbeck, Isaac)
Wolf, William (Wolf, William)
Woolcart, Gideon (Woolcot, Gideon)
Wright, Bazeleel (Wright, Bezelial)
Wyn, Abraham (Winn, Abraham)
Yeomans, ...ab (not in Fed. Census)

DUANESBURGH
Acorns, ... (Ackins, Samuel)
Ada(ms), Parmenus (Adams, Parmenias)
Adams, Permeny (Adams, Permeny)
Becoff, Aaron (not in Fed. Census)
Beebe, Martin (Beebe, Martin)
Beebe, Reyel (Beebe, Royal)
Blunt, William (Blunt, William)
Bond, ... (Bond, John)
Bond, ... (Bond, Richard)
Brewer, Richard (Brewer, Richard)
Carpenter, Abraham (Carpenter, Abraham)
Carter, John (Carter, John)
Chancey, ... (Chancey, Josiah)

Chapman, ... (Chapman, Daniel)
Clark, Caleb (Clark, Caleb)
Clark, Cornelius (Clark, Cornelius)
Colegrove, ... (Colegrove, Stephen)
Corkins, Abraham (Corkins, Abraham)
Corkins, Jonathan (Corkins, Jonathan)
Cowen, ... non est (not in Fed. Census)
Crandall, ... (Crandell, Eber)
Danolds, Samuel (Daniels, Samuel)
Darling, John (Darling, John)
Davis, Philander (Davis, Philander)
Delong, ... (Delong; Elias)
Drew, Ephraim (Drew, Ephraim)
Eaton, Aaron (Eaton, Aaron)
Eaton, Eleazer (Eaton, Eleazer)
Eaton, ... (Eaton, Emanuel)
Eldridge, Edward (Eldridge, Edward)
Eldridge, Elihu (Eldridge, Elihu)
Forbush, ... (Forbus, Abraham)
Gage, Mortimer (Gage, Mortimer)
Granler, John (Grantier, John)
Hancock, ... (Hanike, Emanuel)
Herick, ... (Herrick, Joseph)
Herick, ... (Herrick, Nathan)
Hill, ... (Hill, Oliver)
Holbert, Reuben (Holbert, Reuben)
Hourd, Earl (Howard, Earl)
Kimbel, Daniel (Kemble, Daniel)
Knap, Peter (Knap, Peter)
Lynd, John (Lynd, John)
(Mc)Lane, ... (McLane, John)
Moore, William (Moore, William)
Moreson, ... (Morrison, Daniel)
North, William (North, William)
Northrup, ... (Northrup, Joel)
Owens, Daniel (Owens, Daniel)
Parsons, John (Parsons, John)
Pattern, ... (Patten, Silas)
Perkins, Daniel B. (Perkins, Daniel B.)
Pitcher, ... (Pitcher, Benjamin)
Pomrey, Seth (Pomroy, Seth)
Purdy, Jeremiah (Purdy, Jeremiah)
Rechter, Nicholas (Richter, Nicholas)
Reed, ... (Reed, Joel)
Richter, Michael (Richter, Michael)
Rockwell, ... (Rockwell, James)
(Roof), Christian (Roof, Christian)
Settle, Jacob (Settle, Jacob)
Shoot, Andrew (Shoot, Andrew)
Smith, Daniel (Smith, Daniel)
Snider, ... (Snyder, Henry)
Snider, ... (Snyder, Philip)
Snyder, Lodewick (Snyder, Lodowick)
Stafford, Ichabod (Stafford, Ichabod)

Stafford, William (Stafford, William)
Stafford, William, Junr (Stafford, William, Junr)
Stanard, (Jos)eph (Stanard, Joseph)
Stevens, Giles (Stephens, Giles)
Styles, ... (Styles, Moses)
Thompson, Banijah (Thompson, Benajah)
Thompson, ... (Thompson, Joel)
Tower, Isaiah (Tower, Isaiah)
Trip, Calvin (Trip, Calvin)
Waterhouse, Josiah (Waterhouse, Josiah)
Westley, Ralph (Westley, Ralph)
Wood, Joseph (Wood, Joseph)
Young, ... (Young, James)

FREEHOLD
Ackley, Elephalet (Ackley, Eliphalet)
Amsden, Simon (Amsden, Simeon)
Avery, ... (Avery, James)
Avery, William (Avery, William)
Baldwin, ... (Baldwin, Abiel)
Baldwin, Curtis (Baldwin, Curtis)
Baldwin, ... (Baldwin, Jonathan)
Barker, ... (Barker, ...)
Barker, Phinehas (Barker, Phenias)
Barker, William (Barker, William)
(B)artle, ... (Bartle, David)
Bartlet, Edmond (Bartlet, Edmund)
Baslee, ... (Basley, Bernard)
Basley, Cutting (Bagsley, Cutting)
Been, ... non est
Bidwell, Benjamin (Bidwell, Benjamin)
Blair, John (Blair, John)
Blin, John (Blin, John)
Boomhoward, ... (Boomhoward, Augustus)
Bracket, Ebenezer (Bracket, Ebenezer)
Brant, Hendrick (Brant, Hendrick)
Brown, (Dan)iel (Brown, Daniel)
Brown, Ichabod (Brown, Ichabod)
Brown, Samuel (Brown, Samuel)
Brownson, Seth (Brownson, Seth)
Bryan, Elijah (Bryant, Elijah)
Bryan, Fowler (Bryant, Fowler)
Bunel, Abraham (Bunnel, Abraham)
Burdeck, Thomas (Burdeck, Thomas)
Canfield, Phinehas (Canfield, Phenias)
Carter, Jacob (Carter, Jacob)
Carter, Thomas (Carter, Thomas)
Cartland, Daniel (Kirtland, Daniel)
Choisley, ... (Chrisley, Peter)
Chryler, Fredrick (Chryster, Frederick)
Claflin, Increase (Claflin, Increase)
Clow, Casper (Clow, Casper)
Concklin, Joseph (Concklin, Joseph)
Cook, Aaron (Cook, Aaron)

Cook, Caleb (Cook, Caleb)
Cook, James (Cook, James)
Cook, Miles (Cook, Miles)
Cook, Moses (Cook, Moses)
Cornwell, Dan (Cornwell, Dan)
Cowles, Eber (Cowles, Eber)
Cowles, John (Cowles, John)
Cowles, Salmon (Cole, Salmon)
Culver, Timothy (Culver, Timothy)
Curtis, Josiah (Curtis, Josiah)
Decker, ... (Decker, Benjamin)
De Silvey, ... (Silvey, Joseph D.)
Dickesson, Joseph (Dickinson, Joseph)
Dudley, Peter (Dudley, Peter)
Dudley, Peter, Junr (Dudley, Peter, Junr)
Duewit, Luke (De Witt, Luke)
Duewit, Luke, Junr (Dewitt, Luke, Junr)
Frusher, ...
George, Thomas (George, Thomas)
Gideons, John (Gideons, John)
Graham, Joseph (Graham, Joseph)
Halenbeek, William (Hallenbeck, William)
Harriete, Thomas (Harriett, Thomas)
Harrison, John (Harrison, John)
Heart, Elihau (Hart, Elihu)
Heart, Joseph (Hart, Joseph)
Herton, David (Horton, David)
Homan, John (Homan, John)
Hotchkiss, Samuel (Hotchkiss, Samuel)
Howe, Joshua (How, Joshua)
Hubbard, Arunah (Hubbard, Arunal)
Huse, Bodwell (Huse, Bodwell)
Jewil, David (Jewell, David)
(Jo)hnson, ... (Johnston, Paul)
Knowles, Thomas (Knowles, Thomas)
Linsby, Abraham (Lindsey, Abraham)
Lord, Asa (Lord, Asa)
Mitchel, (A)nan (Mitchell, Anan)
Moon, John (Moon, John)
Nelson, Jonathan (Nelson, Jonathan)
Norton, Ambruas (Norton, Ambross)
Norton, Asher (Norton, Asher)
Norton, Daniel (Norton, Daniel)
Norton, Elan (Norton, Elan)
Olmsted, Nemiah (Olmsted, Nehemiah)
Pain, Eli (Paine, Eli)
Painter, ... (Painter, Edward)
Palmer, John (Palmer, John)
Passivee, Timothy (Purcival, Timothy)
Patree, Henry (Patric, Henry)
Pearce, John (Pearee, John)
Peasee, ... (Pease, John)
Perry, ... (Perry, Tolbert)
Phelp, Israel (Phelps, Israel)

Phelps, Stephen (Phelps, Stephen)
Plank, Johannis (Plank, illegible)
Platt, Stephen (Platt, Stephen)
Post, Ezre (Post, Ezra)
Powers, Ephraim (Powers, Ephraim)
Pratt, Agustus (Pratt, Augustus)
Pratt, Beriah (Pratt, Beriah)
Pratt, ... (Pratt, Jonathan)
Rowley, Moses (Rowley, Moses)
Rude, Asa (Rude, Asa)
Rundell, Joseph, Junr (Rundell, Josepn, Junr)
Runole, Reuben (Rundle, Reuben)
Sage, David (Sage, David)
Semorson, Christopher non est
Shepard, ... (Sheppard, John)
Shew, Agustine (Shew, Agustine)
Showaman, John (Showaman, John)
Skeel, Adonirom (Skeel, Adanirom)
Smith, Benjamin (Smith, Benjamin)
Smith, Caleb (Smith, Caleb)
Smith, Hendrick (Smith, Hendrick)
Smith, Jacob (Smith, Jacob)
Smith, James (Smith, James)
Smith, Jared (Smith, Jared)
Smith, Jared, Junr (Smith, Jared, Junr)
Smith, Thomas (Smith, Thomas)
Smith, Thomas (Smith, Thomas)
Snideker, James (Snidecker, James)
Stanard, Eliakim (Stanard, Eliakim)
Stanley, ... (Stanley, Richard)
Stockin, (Step)hen (Stocking, Stephen)
Stoks, Jonatha (Stokes, Jonathan)
Stone, Ichial (Stone, Johial)
Striker, ... (Stryker, Barent)
(S)triker, ... (Stryker, Peter)
Strong, Bala (Strong, Selah)
Strong, Bela, Junr (Strong, Selah, Junr)
Strong, Elikem (Strong, Elikem)
Strong, Selah (Strong, Selah)
Strope, Jacob (Strope, Jacob)
Summers, David (Summers, David)
Thorp, Aaron (Tharp, Aaron)
Thorp, Amos (Tharp, Amos)
Towsey, Lerah (Towsey, Serah)
Trusdale, William (Truesdale, William)
Trusdale, William, Junr (Truesdale, William, Junr)
Tyler, Elisha (Tyler, Elisha)
Vallance, Azariah (Vallance, Azariah)
Vanloke, John (Van Loon, John)
Vining, Rosinah (Vining, Rosena)
Voorhil, ... (Voorhees, Roelif)
Wadams, ... (Waddams, Caleb)
Wilcox, Francis (Wilcocks, Francis)
Wright, George (Wright, George)

Wright, Joab (Wright, Joab)
Wright, John (Wright, John)
Wright, Semeon (Wright, Simeon)
(Wr)ightmyer, ... (Wrightmyer, George)
Wrightmyer, ... (Wrightmyer, illegible)

HALFMOON
Adson, Adam (Edson, Adam)
Atwell, ...d (Atwell, Richard)
Baits, George (Baits, George
Baker, Seth (Baker, Seth)
Barns, Comfort (Barns, Comfort)
Barns, Iziah (Barns, Isiah)
Barns, ... (Barns, James)
Barns, John (Barns, John)
Barns, Lewis (Barns, Lewis)
Beaker, Peter (Baker, Peter)
Bell, Gerrit (Bell, Gerrit)
Berry, John (Berry, John)
Bethey, Preserved (Beth, Preserved)
Blancher, ... (Blancher, Ephraim)
Bonard, ... (Bonord, Eli)
Bradshaw, William (Bradshaw, Willm)
Bratt, Dirck (Bredt, Derick)
Bratt, Gertrude (Bradt, Gertrude)
Bratt, Margaret (Bradt, Margaret)
Brayton, William (Brayton, Willm)
Brevot, Henry (Brevoort, Henry)
Bromsen, Samuel (Bronson, Samuel)
Brown, Nathan (Brown, Nathan)
Brown, ... (Brown, Valentine)
Bruer, Jeremiah (Brewer, Jeremiah)
Buck, John (Bock, John)
Bull, Amos (Buel, Amos)
Burhns, John (Burns, John)
Burtos, Richard (Burtis, Richard)
Bush, John (Bush, John)
Buskerk, John (Buskirk, John)
Buskerk, Joseph (Buskirk, Joseph)
Buys, James (Berys, James)
Chadwell, James (Chadwell, Sinson)
Cleveland, Ezekiel (Cleveland, Ezekiel)
Cleveland, Josiah (Cleveland, Josiah)
Cloe, James (Clow, James)
Close, ... (Close, Gideon)
Clout, Jacob (Clute, Jacob)
Clute, Gerardus (Clute, Gradus)
Clute, Gradus (Clute, Gradas, Ju)
Clute, Gradus J. (Illute, Gradus)
Comstock, Aron (Comstack, Aaron)
Concken, ... (Conklin, Abigal)
Concklen, Elizabeth (Conklin, Elizabeth)
Concklen, Thomas (Conklin, Thomas)
Concklen, Thomas, Junr (Conklin, Thomas, Ju^r)

Conner, John (Conner, John)
Conrell, ...hn (Cornale, John)
Cortes, Edward (Carter, Edward)
Cramer, George, Junr (Cramer, George, J^r)
Crossman, Dan (Crossman, Daniel)
Crudes, John (Cruden, John)
Curden, John (Cuerden, John)
Darbee, ... (Darber, Edward)
Darbee, John (Derbe, John)
Darbee, (Jon)athan (Darbey, Jonathan)
Darbeshere, Daniel (Derbeshire, Daniel)
Darbeshere, James (Derbeshire, James)
Davis, ... (Davis, Henry)
Degrouf, ... (De Graaff, Abraham)
Delong, Daniel (Delong, Daniel)
Demilt, Isaac (De Milt, Isaac)
Demon, George (Demmen, George)
Denwerken, John K. (V: De Werken, John H.)
Depue, Elias (Depue, Elias)
Devoe, Isaac (Devoe, Isaac)
Devoe, Samuel (Devoe, Samuel)
Devow, Martinus (De Vow, Martinus)
Diett/Dutt/Drett (?), John (Drett, John)
Dingman, Abraham (Dingman, Abraham)
Dob, Johannis (Dob, Johannis)
Dobt, Johannis (Dobt, Johannis)
Donaldson, John (Donaldson, John)
Donnels, John (Daniels, John)
Doty, Philip (Doty, Philip)
Drommond, John (Drummin, John)
Duel, Abraham (Dellin, Abraham)
Duning, Ephraim (Dunning, Ephraim)
Efner, Henry (Effnor, Henry)
Eldrid, Robert (Eldridge, Robert)
Evans, Edward (Evins, Edward)
Evans, Andrew (Evins, Andrew)
Evens, Nathan (Evins, Nathan)
Fackner, Peter (Faulkner, Peter)
Fisher, John (Fisher, John)
Fitchbut, Isaac (Fitchbut, Isaac)
Forsburk, Dirck (Vosburgh, Dirck)
Forsburk, Peter (Vosburgh, Peter)
Fort, John (Fort, John)
Fort, Nicholas (Fort, Nicholas)
Fransisco, Francis (Fransisco, Francis)
Frasier, William H. (Frazier, Willm)
Free, Ezekiel (Free, Ezekiel)
Fuller, ... (Fuller, Isaiah)
Garnsey, Nathan (Guernsey, Nathan)
Gilberts, ... (Gilberts, Joseph)
Gilderslaf, ... (Gilderslea, Elkanah)
Given, ... (Ginin, John)
Goodrich, Gilbert (Goodrich, Gilbert)
Goslen, William (Goslin, Willm)

Grigs, Simon (Griggs, Simon)
Grogory, Matthew (Gidory, Mathew)
Groom, David (Groom, David)
Gue, John (Gus, John)
(Hals)tead, ... (Halsted, James)
Halstead, (Tim)othy (Halsted, Timothy)
Hamilton, John (Hamilton, John)
Hanyons, Gerrit (Hanyons, Gerrit)
Harris, William (Harris, Will[m])
Hazard, Samuel (Hazzard, Samuel)
Heemstraet, Dirck (Hemstraat, Derrich)
Hegeman, Adrian (Hegerman, Adriah)
Henda, Zebulon (Handre, Zebulon)
Hix, Samuel (Hiras, Samuel)
Holmes, Lyenges (Holmes (Lycurgus)
Holmes, Nathaniel (Helmer, Nath[l])
Holmes, Reuben (Helmer, Ruben)
Holsted, Laurence (Halsted, Lawrence)
Homen, Phines (Hammond, Phineas)
Hopsher, John (Hopaker, John)
Howard, John (Howard, John)
Hybert, Jabes (Huybert, Jabez)
James, Mahanel (James, Nath[l])
Jones, Samuel (Jones, Samuel)
Kaler, Isaac (Keeler, Isaac)
Karr, James (Kerr, James)
Karr, John (Kerr, John)
Ketchum, Hezekiah (Ketchem, Hezekiah)
Kinian, Carnar (Kenyon, Gardiner)
Knight, James (Knight, James)
Knowlton, John (Knowlton, John)
Ladow, ... (Ladaw, Stephen)
Lansing, John (Lansing, John)
Leach, Jacob (Lush, Joseph)
Lint, Moses (Lent, Moses)
McConnel, Christopher (McConnel, Cristopher)
McCourtie, John (McCourtis, John)
McCoy, William (McCoy, Will[m])
McCready, David (McCrady, David)
McGee, James (McGee, James)
McNeal, Arch (McNeil, Archibald)
McNeal (McNell, John)
Mapes, Phineas (Mapes, Phineas)
Marchouse, Abel (Morehouse, Abel)
Merrihue, ... (Merriheu, David)
Miller, Jacob (Miller, Jacob)
Miller, John (Miller, John)
Miller, John (Miller, John)
Mix, (Benja)min (Mix, Benj[n])
Monsie, John (Monsey, John)
Morkie/ Markie, Rulif (Markie, Rulif)
Morse, Amos (Moss, Amos)
Mosher, Joseph (Mosher, Joseph)
Murrey, ... (Murry, Gilbert)

Northup, Samuel (Nortrup, Samuel)
Oliphant, Dunken (Oliphant, Duncan)
Oringer, Martinus (Oringer, Martinus)
Ostrander, Abraham (Ostranda, Abraham)
Ostrander, Evert (Ostranda, Evert)
Ostrander, Jacobus (Ostranda, Jacobus)
Ostrander, ... (Ostranda, Peter)
Ouderkerk, (Abra)ham (Onderkirk, Abraham)
Ouderkerk, ...is (Andeshank, Johannis)
Palmer, Ebenezer (Palmer, Ebenezer)
Parsa, James (Pierce, James)
Pattit, John (Pettit, John)
Peasall, James (Pearsall, James)
Peek, (Jos)eph (Peck, Joseph)
Perrish, Samuel (Parrish, Samuel)
Per Voort, Mary (Brevoort, Mary)
Peters, ... (Peters, Richard)
Peterson, Isaac (Peterson, Isaac)
Picket, Stephen (Pickett, Stephen)
Porter, ...nel (Porter, Nathl)
Pourter, Amos (Porter, Amos)
Powell, ... (Powell, Jonathan)
Powell, ... (Powell, Morgan)
Powell, ... (Powell, Willm)
Quackenboss, Jacob (Quackenbush, Jacob)
Quackenbush, Abraham (Quackenbush, Abraham)
Quivey, John (Quincy, John)
Rano, Francis (Reno, Francis)
Reed, ... (Reed, Daniel)
Roberts, Ichabod (Roberts, Ichabod)
Robins, Joseph (Robins, Joseph)
Rogers, Jedediah (Rogers, Jedediah)
Root, Asa (Root, Asa)
Rosekram, Benjamin (Rosekrans, Benjn)
Rout, Benjamin (Root, Benjn)
Ruger, Gabril (Reiger, Gabriel)
Sackrider, (Timo)thy (Sackrider, Timothy)
Sact, James (Sweet, James)
Schoten, (Ephr)aim (Scoutan, Ephraim)
Schott, Moses (Schatt, Moses)
Scouten, Abraham (Scouten, Abraham)
Scouten, John (Scouten, John)
Senot, Patrick (Sennet, Patrick)
Seouton, Simon (Scouten, James)
Sharter, Felox (Shuster, Felix)
Shear, Patris (Shier, Petrus)
Shier, Andries (Shier, Andreas)
Shier, Andries, Junr (Shier, Andreas, Ju^r)
Shier, John (Shier, John)
Shier, Silvanus (Shier, Silvanus)
Shepherd, Daniel (Shephard, Daniel)
Shepherd, Russell (Shephard, Russell)
Shepherd, William (Shephard, Willm)
Sibley, Joseph (Sibley, Joseph)

Sickle, Philip F. (Funssickle, Philip)
Simons, ... (Simmons, Andrus)
Smith, John (Smith, John)
Smith, John (Smith, John)
Smith, Joseph (Smith, Joseph)
Smith, Samuel (Smith, Samuel)
Smith, Timothy (Smith, Timothy)
Smith, Ti(mothy) (Smith, Timothy)
Spiers, Joseph (Spiers, Joseph)
Spink, Samuel (Spink, Samuel)
Standish, Cyrus (Standish, Cyrus)
Steenbergh, Elias (Steenbergh, Elias)
Steenbergh, John (Steenbergh, John)
Steenbergh/Steenberg, Peter (Strenbergh, Peter)
Stenbergh, Jacob (Steenbergh, Jacob)
Stenbergh, James (Steenbergh, James)
Swartwout, John (Swortevant, John)
Sweetland, Samuel (not in Fed. Census)
Swezey/Sweney, Joseph (Swaesy, Joseph)
Taller, William (Tiller, Willm)
Tarpening, Jacob (Terpenny, Jacob)
Tarpening, John (Terpenny, John)
Tarpening, John, Junr (Terpenny, John, J^r)
Tarpening, Peter (Terpenny, Peter)
Tarpening, Samuel (Terpenny, Samuel)
Tater, Reuben, Junr (Taylor, Ruben, Ju^r)
Tayler, Ruben (Taylor, Ruben)
Taylor, Ezekiel (Taylor, Ezekiel)
Taylor, John (Taylor, John)
Taylor, Joshua (Taylor, Joshua)
Taylor, Josiah (Taylor, Josiah)
Teachout, John (Tichout, John)
Teachout, William (Tichhout, Willm)
Teed, Samuel (Todd, Lemuel)
Teller, Remson (Teller, Remson)
Ten Broeck, Hannah (Ten Broock, Hannah)
Thompson, John (Thompson, John)
Tice/Tin, Joseph (Tice, Joseph)
Tichout, ... (Tichout, Cornelius)
Tittore, Peter (Tilton, Peter)
Travis, Abraham (Travis, Abraham)
Trip, Calep (Trip, Caleb)
Trip, Evert (Trip, Evert)
Trip, William (Trip Willm)
Ulis, John (Hees, John)
Vandenbergh, ... (V:De Bergh, Maika)
Van Denbergh, ... (V:De Bergh, Moses)
Van Denbergh, ... (V:De Bergh, Nicholas)
Van Denbogert, Myndert (V:De Bogert, Mindert)
V^n Derheyden, Nanning (V:Der Heydon, Nanning)
Van Dewater, Frans (V:De Waterm Frens)
V. De Werken, John (V. De Werken, John)
V^n Dewerken, Mary (V:De Werkem, Mary)
V^n Dewerken, William (V:De Werken, Willm)

Van Hyning, Hendrich (Van Hyning, Hendrich)
Van Ness, Antie (V:Ness, Antie)
(Van Scho)onhoven, ... (V:Schoonhaven, Guest.)
(Van Sch)oonhoven, ... (Van Schoonhaven, Jacobus)
Vn Vleck, ...anous (V:Vleck, Mannus)
Vn Vranken, Adam (V:Vranken, Adam)
Vn Vranken, Adam, Junr (V:Vranken, Adam, Jur)
Van Vranken, Gerrit (V:Vranken, Gerrit)
Vn Vranken, Gertrude (V. Vranken, Gertrude)
Van Vranken, Jane (V:Vranken, Janatie)
Van Vranken, John (V:Vranken, Johannis)
Vn Vranken, Maria (V:Vranken, Maria)
Vn Woert, Eldert (V:Woort, Eldert)
Viel, ... (Viele, Isaac)
Vincent, Jeremiah (Vincent, Jeremiah)
Visscher, Eldert (Visher, Eldert)
Visscher, Nicholas (Visher, Nicholas)
Wackenbush, Gerardus (Quakenbush, Gerardus)
Waite, Oliver (Wait, Oliver)
Walderon, Gerrit (Waldron, Gerrit)
Waldo, ... (Waldo, Shubael)
Waldron, John (Waldron, John)
Way, David (Wey, David)
Wever, Edward (Weaver, Edward)
Wilbur, Gideon, Junr (Wilber, Gideon, Junr)
Wilcox, Martin (Wilcox, Martin)
Wilde, John (Wilde, John)
Wilde, Stephen (Wilde, Stephen)
Williams, John (Williams, John)
Williams, Samuel (Williams, Samuel)
Williams, Samuel (Williams, Samuel)
Williams, William (Williams, Willm)
Williams, William, Junr (Williams, William, Jr)
Willsie, William (Wilse, Willm)
Wood, David (Wood, David)
Woodard, David (Woodward, David)
Wooden, Reuben (Woodin, Rubin)
Wright, Henry (Waight, Henry)
Young, Daniel (Young, Daniel)
Young, Daniel (Youngs, Daniel)

HOOSICK
Abbott, Joel (Abbott, Joel)
Allen, ... (Allen, Jeremiah)
Allen, Stepn (Allen, Stephen)
Andrews, ... (Andrews, Philemon)
Ash, John, Junr (Ash, John, Junr)
Ashley, Zenus (Ashley, Zeners)
Ashly, Elkany (Ashley, Elkanah)
Ashworth, Andrew (Elsworth, Andrew)
Ball, Abraham (Ball, Abraham)
Ball, Deborah (Ball, Deborah)
Barnet, ... (Barnett, James)
Barnet, ... (Barnett, Moses)

Barnet, ... (Barnett, Nath[l])
Barnhart, ... (Barnhart, Henry)
Barnhart, ... (Barnhart, Joseph)
Barton, ... (Burton, Isaiah)
Bater, John (Bates, John)
Bates, ... (Bates, James)
Bebe, Isaac (Beebe, Isaac)
Blakely, Jonathan (Blakely, Jonathan)
Blass, Jn[o] (Bliss, John)
Bly, Asa (Bly, Asa)
Bovee, Peter (Bovee, Peter)
Bovie, Gerret (Bovee, Gerrit)
Bovie, ... (Bovee, Jacob)
Bovie, Mattice (Bovee, Mathew)
Bovie, ... (Bovee, Philip)
Braiy, ... (Bailey, Israel)
Bratt, Bernardus (Bradt, Bernard)
Bratt, Daniel B. (Bradt, Daniel B.)
Bratt, Garrit (Bratt, Gerrit)
Breese, Henry (Bresser, Henry)
Brewer, ... (Brewer, Mathew)
Briggs, ... (Briggs, Will[m])
Brown, Nath[l] (Brown, Nath[l])
Brown, Nicholas (Powers, Nicholas)
Brown, Rufas (Brown, Rufus)
Browning, ... (Browning, Will[m])
Brunsen, ... (Brunsen, Josiah)
Bruse, Garrit (Bresse, Gerrit T.)
Bruster, W[m] (Brewster, Will[m])
Bull, Abraham, Jun[r] (Bull, Abraham, Ju[r])
Bull, Isaac (Bull, Israel)
Bunday, Elisha (Bundy, Elisha)
Bunday, Simeon (Bundy, Simon)
Burdick, ... (Burdick, Josiah)
Bussey, ... (Bussey, Thomas)
(Bu)tler, ... (Butler, Thomas)
Calf, Charles (Coff, Charles)
Calf, Frederick (Coff, Frederik)
Calf, William (Coff, Will[m])
Card, Samuel (Card, Samuel)
Card, Thomas (Card, Thomas)
Carlton, ... (Carleton, Sarah)
(Car)penter, ... (Carpenter, Jacob)
Carr, William (Kerr, Will[m])
Carter, Gerard (Carter, Girard)
Carter, Samuel (Carter, Samuel)
Case, Jonath[n] (Case, Jonathan)
Case, Oliver (Case, Oliver)
(C)hapel, ... (Chappel, Samuel)
(C)hase, ... (Chace, John)
Chase, Lemuel (Chase, Lemuel)
Chase, Nathan (Chase, Nathan)
Chase, Nathan (Chase, Nathan, Ju[r])
Chase, Wing (Chace, Wing)

Clark, Henry (Clark, Henry)
Clark, James (Clerk, James)
Cole, Asa (Cole, Asa)
Cole, William (Caley, Willm)
Coller, Elisha (Coller, Eliaha)
Collier, Willm (Colliar, Willm)
Collor, ..., Junr (Caller, Elisha, Junr)
Compton, John (Compton, John)
Coon, Jonath^{n} (Coon, Jonathan)
Costle, Daniel (Castles, Daniel)
Covey, John (Covey, John)
Covil, ... (Covill, Richard)
Cronkite, Jacob (Cronkhite, Jacob)
Cross, ... (Cross, Ebenezer)
Culler, ... (Cutler, Samuel)
Cumpstock, Jno (Comstock, John)
Cumpstock, Theop^{s} (Comstock, Theophilus)
Cunningham, ... (Cunningham, Layton)
Curler, Henry (Cusler, Henry)
Curtis, ... (Custin, Stephen)
(C)usten, ... (Custin, John)
Darling, ... (Darling, Abner)
Darr, Joseph (Dorr, Joseph)
Daught, Jno (Dought, John)
Davis, Thomas (Davis, Thomas)
Day, Noah (Dey, Noah)
Dean, ... (Dean, Seth)
Denn, (D)ennis (Dunn, Dennis)
Dewey, Isaiah (Dewery, Isaiah)
Dickerson, ... (Drinkwater, Samuel)
(Di)ckerson, ... (Dickison, Samuel G.)
Dickeson, ... (Deckison, Gideon)
(Do)naldson, ... (Donaldson, Essick)
Dor, Mathew (Dorr, Mathew)
Doreman, Christopher (Dorman, Christopher)
(Dr)inkwater, ... (Drinkwater, Samuel)
Dunslow, James (Dinslow, James)
Dutcher, Abrah^{m} (Decker, Abraham)
Eady, Elisha (Eddy, Elisha)
Ellit, ... (Ellet, John)
Farrier, David (Ferris, David)
Fields, Joseph (Fields. Joseph)
Frazier, W^{m} (Frazier, Willm)
French, Jno (French, John)
Frink, Asa (Frink, Asa)
Frink, Luke (Frink, Luke)
Frink, Nathan (Frink, Nathan)
Frink, Theophilus (Frink, Theophilus)
Funda, Jno D. (Fonda, John D.)
Gaffin, James (Griffin, James)
Gallop, ... (Gallop, Jesse)
Gallop, William (Gallop, Willm)
Ganoe, John (Gano, John)

(Gard)ner, ... (Gardner, Josiah)
Goes, Mathew (Goes, Mathew)
Graves, Dyer (Graves, Dyer)
Gray, ...zel (Grey, Hazael)
Green, Christ^r (Green, Cristopher)
Green, Jeremiah (Green, Jeremiah)
(G)reen, ... (Green, Thomas)
Griffen, Samuel (Griffin, John)
Griffith, Paul (Griffths, Paul)
(Gri)swold, ... (Griswold, Daniel)
Grosen, ... (Grogan, Patrick)
Haines, Philip (Harris, Philip)
Hallenbeek, ... (Hallenbeck, Daniel)
Hartwell, ... (Hartwell, Thomas)
(Ha)viland, ... (Haviland, Garrison)
(Hav)iland, ... (Haviland, James)
(Hav)iland, ... (Haviland, John)
Haynes, Edmond (Harris, Edmond)
Herrington, ... (Herrington, Silas)
Hewitt, Simeon (Hurt, Simon)
Hicks, Moses (Hicks, Moses)
Hill, ... (Hill, John)
Hill, ..., Junr (Hill, John, Junr)
Hill, Samuel D. (Hull, Samuel D.)
Hill, ... (Hill, Thomas)
Hillen, William (Helm, Willm)
Hillen, William, Junr (Helm, Willm, J^r)
Hobson, Simon (Hobson, Simon)
Hodges, (Ez)ekiel (Hodges, Ezekiel)
Hodges, ... (Hodges, Mathew)
(Ho)dges, ... (Hodges, Samuel)
Hogle, Abraham (Hazel, Abraham)
Hogle, ... (Hazel, Francis)
Horton, ... (Horton, Lewis)
Howard, Thomas (Howard, Thomas)
Howk, Widow (Heryck, Mary)
Humphrey, Russel (Humphrey, Russel)
Ingerson, Jno (Ingerson, John)
Johnson, ... (Johnson, Elkanah)
Johnson, Rufus (Johnson, Rufus)
Jones, Rufas (Jones, Rufus)
Jones, ... (Jones, Zebulon)
(Kid)digan, ... (Kiddigan, Berney)
Kinyan, Robert (Kenyon, Robert)
Kinyon, ... (Kenyon, John)
Kronkite, ... (Cronkhite, John)
Kronkite, ... (Cronkhite, Stephen)
Lake, ... (Lake, Gerrit T£)
Lake, Henry (Lake, Henry)
Lake, ... (Lake, Henry T.)
Lake, ... (Looks, James)
Lamb, ... (Lamb, Isaac)
Lampman, Jno (Lampman, John)
Lansing, Isaac H. (Lansing, Isaac H.)

Larbe, Nathaniel (Laraby, Nathl)
Lewis, Benjam^n (Lewis, Benjn)
Lewis, Henry (Lewis, Henry)
Lewis, Jno (Lewis, John)
Little, ... (Little, Henry)
Lutteridge, Thomas (Lotridge, Thomas)
McCarty, ... (McCarty, Dennis)
McCoy, William (McCoy, Willm)
McGowan, James (McGowan, James)
Marble, John (Marble, John)
Mark, ... (Mark, Ephraim)
Markell, Teunis (Merkell, Thunis)
Marsh, Amos (Marsh, Amos)
Matheson, ... (Mattison, Ezekiel)
Mattison, ... (Mattison, Isiah)
Mattison, Jno (Mattison, John)
Mayley, ... (Migley, John)
Miller, Aaron (Miller, Aaron)
Miller, Levi (Miller, Levi)
Milliman, ... (Milliman, Rowland)
(Mill)iman, ... (Milliman, Thomas)
Minter, ... (Minter, Felix)
Monser, Benjamin (Monger, Benjn)
Moore, ... (Moore, Willm)
Moshier, Samuel (Mosher, Samuel)
Mosier, Edward (Mosher, Edward)
Mosier, ... (Mosher, Wilcox)
Mosley, ... (Moseley, Jacob)
Mosley, ... (Mosely, Jonathan)
Munroe, ... (Monroe, John)
Murfey, Thomas (Murphy, Thomas)
Newell, ... (Newell, David)
Newell, ... (Newell, Joseph)
Nichols, ... (Nichols, Caleb)
Nichols, ... (Nichols, George)
Nichols, ... (Nichols, John)
Nichols, ... (Nichols, Nathan)
Nichols, ... (Nichols, Rowland)
Nicklison, ... (Nicholson, Israel)
Niles, ... (Niles, Samuel)
Ostrander, Abraham (Ostranda, Abraham)
Ostrander, Peter V. (Ostranda, Peter)
Ouderkerk, Fred^k (Onderkirk, Frederick)
Oderkerk, Jacob (Onderkirk, Jacob)
Ouderkerk, Jno (Onderkirk, John)
Outlip, Christian (Outlip, Cristopher)
Pachen, Zebulon (Patchin, Zebulon)
Palmer, ... (Palmer, John)
Palmer, ... (Palmer, Stephen)
Parker, ... (Parker, Caleb)
Parks, Rufus (Parks, Rufus)
Parsons, Aaron (Parsons, Aaron)
Patting, ... (Patten, Joseph)
Pearse, Michael (Pierce, Mial)

Pigsley, ... (Pigsley, Elijah)
Porter, John (Porter, John)
Porter, John (Porter, John)
Powell, Richard (Powel, Richard)
Powell, Thomas (Powel, Thomas)
Price, Jn⁰ (Price, John)
Putman, Fran^s (Putman, Francis)
Quackenboss, John (Quakenbush, John)
Rase (or Race?), Widow (Rose, Mary)
Read, Asa (Reid, Asa)
Read, Stephen (Reed, Stephen)
Rich, ... (Rich, Willm)
Richardson, ... (Richardson, James)
Roberts, W^m, Junr (Roberts, Willm, Junr)
Robinson, ... (Robison, Willm)
Robison, Francis (Robison, Francis)
Rockwell, Reuben (Rockwell, Ruben)
Rodgers, Carey (Rogers, Carey)
Rodgers, Clark (Rogers, Clerk)
Rodgers, ... (Rogers, Ishmael)
Rogers, ... (Rogers, Stephen)
Russell, ... (Russel, Solomon)
Ryon, John (Ryan, John)
Sales, John (Sales, John)
Salesbury, ... (Salisberry, Samuel)
Schuyler, Nicholas (Schuyler, Nicholas)
Selah, ... (Selah, Willm)
Shepherd, ... (Shepherd, Benjn)
Shepherd, ... (Shepherd, Jane)
Shulter, Jn⁰ (Shulter, John)
Sickles, Thomas (Sickles, Thomas)
Sickels, Zachiriah W. (Sickles, Zacheriah W.)
Siers, ... (Sears, Richard)
Sisson, Saml (Sisson, Samuel)
Smith, Jacob (Smith, Jacob)
Smith, ... (Smith, Willm)
Snyder, (Henry), Junr (Snider, Henry, Ju^r)
Spencer, Joseph (Spencer, Joseph)
Spencer, ... (Spencer, Michael)
(Sp)rague, ... (Sprague, Eli)
(Sp)rague, ... (Sprague, John)
(Sp)rague, ... (Sprague, Stephen)
Squires, ... (Squires, John)
Starkes, Israel (Starks, Israel)
Starkes, Obadiah (Starks, Obadiah)
(Sti)lson, ... (Stilson, Henry)
Swan, ... (Swan, Nero)
Sweet, ... (Sweet, Jeremiah)
Sweet, ... (Sweet, Simon)
Taylor, Matthew (Taylor, Nathan)
Taylor, Medad (Taylor, Medad)
Thayer, (Ru)ben (Thayre, Ruben)
Tracy, Nathan (Tracy, Nathan)
(Tri)pp, ... (Trip, Lott)

Turner, Isaac (Turner, Isaac)
Turner, Richard (Turner, Richard)
Twiss, Jonathan (Twiss, Jonathan)
Van Buren, John (V:Buren, John)
Van Buren, Matthew (V:Buren, Mathew)
(Van) Buskerck, ... (V:Buskirk, Peter)
(Van) Ness, ... (Van Ness, Jacob)
(Van) Ornum (V:Arnum, Freelove)
(Van Re)nsselaer, ... (V:Rensselaer, David)
Van Sant, William (Van Zandt, Willm)
V(an) Surdam, Samuel (V:Surdam, Samuel)
Van Wormer, John (V:Wormer, John)
Vredenbergh, ... (V:Den Bergh, Abraham)
Vredenbergh, ... (V:Den Bergh, James)
Wait, David (Wait, David)
Wait, ... (Wait, George)
Walker, Henry (Walker, Henry)
Wallace, (Dan)iel (Wallace, Daniel)
Wallace, ... (Wallace, John)
Wallace, ... (Wallace, Timothy)
Wallworth, ... (Walworth, John)
(Wa)rner, ... (Warner, Willm)
Waters, Adam (Waters, Adam)
Waters, Bejalow (Waters, Bigelow)
Watson, ... (Watson, Benjn)
Watson, Solom^n (Watson, Solomon)
Way, Samuel (Wey, Samuel)
Welch, John (Welsh, John)
West, ... (West, Ichabod)
Williams, David (Williams, David)
Williams, Jno (Williams, John)
Williamson, ... (Williamson, James)
Williamson, ... (Williamson, Samuel)
(W)illis, ... (Wills, Zenus)
Wilson, Alexander (Willson, Alex^r)
Witman, Benjn (Pitman, Benjn)
(Wol)worth, ... (Wolworth, Willm)
Wood, Jonath^n (Wood, Jonathan)
Woolen, ... (Wooler, Presberry)
York, David (York, David)

SCHENECTADY
Alexander, Robert (Alexander, Robert)
Ament, Elstert (Ament, Eldert)
Backes, Jacob (Backus, Jacob)
Banker, John (Banker, John)
Banker, Thomas B. (Banker, Thomas B.)
Barheyt, ...
Barheyt, ... (Barheyt, Cornelius)
Barheyt, ... (Barheyt, Jeremiah)
Barheyt, John (Barheyt, John)
Barheyt, ... (Barheyt, John C.)
Barheyt, ... (Barheyt, Lewis)
Barhydt, Mary (Barheyt, Mary)

Bartley, Mary (Bartell, Maria)
Beck, Elizabeth (Bag, Elizabeth)
Becker, ... (Becker, Garrit A.)
Bedsted, Jacob (Bedsteda, Jacob)
Beekman, ... (Beekman, Jacob)
Beth, ... (Betts, Robert)
(B)igham, ...
Black, Robert (Black, Robert)
(B)lackford, ... (Blackfort, Anthony)
Blackney, ...
Bohannen, (Ro)bert (Bohannan, Robert)
Bonnet, ... (not in Fed. Census)
Bonney, Ichabod (Bonny, Ichabod)
Bonney, John (Bonny, John)
Bourk, Charles (Burck, Charles)
Boyd, ... (Boyd, Mary)
Bradford, James (Bradford, James)
Bradt, ... (Bradt, Cornelius)
Brannen, Abraham (Brannen, Abraham)
Bratt, ...
Bratt, ... (Bradt, Aaron S.)
Bratt, (Abr)aham (Bradt, Abraham)
Bratt, ... (Bradt, Frederick)
Bratt, ... (Bradt, Hermanus)
Bratt, ... (Bradt, Jacobus)
Bratt, Samuel A. (Bradt, Samuel A.)
Braughum, Joseph (Brackham, Joseph)
Braughum, Samuel (Brackham, Samuel)
Broughum, John (not in Fed. Census)
Browen, ... (Brownem, Enock)
Brower, Henry (Brower, Henry)
Brower, ... (Brewer, Jellis)
Brown, ...
Brown, Abraham (Brown, Abraham)
Brown, ... (Brown, Henry)
Brown, John (Brown, John)
Brown, John (Brown, John)
Burick, Coonraet (Burick, Conradt)
Burley, John (Burley, John)
Burns, ... (Burns, David)
Calbenson, William (Culberson, William)
Celly, William (Kelly, William)
Channen, ...
Channen, Alexander (Shannan, Alexander)
Channen, George (Channen, George)
Channen, Michael (Shannan, Michael)
Christians, Ahasuerus (Crestianse, Ahasuerus)
Christians, Isaa (Crestianse, Isaac)
Clute, ... (Clute, Bartholomew)
Clute, ... (Clute, Jacob)
Clute, ... P. (Clute, Jacob P.)
Clute, ... (Clute, John)
Clute, ... (Clute, John Baptist)
Clute, ... (Clute, John I.)

```
Colhuyt, Abraham (Oathoudt, Abraham)
Collins, ... (Collins, James)
Conner, Lanester (Conner, LancasTer)
Consalus, ... (Komsalsales, David)
Coon, Timo(thy) (Coon, Timothy)
Corl, ... (Carl, Andrew)
Corl, ... (Carl, John)
Corn, ... (Corn, William)
Coughran, ... (Caughoon, Hugh)
Cown, ... (Cown, Peter)
Crawford, John, assessor (Cranford, John)
Cummins, Joseph (Cummins, Joseph)
Dance, ... (Danee, Ealter)
Davis, William (not in Fed. Census)
Day, Elias (Day, Elias)
Degroff, ... (De Groff, Abraham)
Degroff, Andries (De Graaf, Andreas)
(De)groff, ... (De Grove, Catlintea)
De Groff, ... (De Graaf, Claus)
D Groff, Cornelius (Degrove, Cornelius)
Delmonth, Abraham (Dalmond, Abraham)
Delmonth, Henry (Delmonth, Henry)
Deviear, Da(nie)l (Darrah, Daniel)
Dinning, John (not in Fed. Census)
Donnon, Grissel (Donnan, Crissel)
Dorn, John (Dorn, John)
Dovener, William (Devener, Will$^m$)
Dowen, John (Dowan, John)
Duning, Abel (Dunning, Able)
Dunlap, ... (Dunlap, James)
Eads, Joseph (Edes, Joseph)
Erkson, ... (Arkson, John)
Fanal, Canada (Ferrell, Kenedy)
Filkins, James (Filkins, James)
Flagg, ... (Flagg, John)
Forgeson, John (Ferguson, John)
France, Benjamin (not in Fed. Census)
Franck, ... (Frank, David)
Freemen, ... (Freeman, John)
Frymine, (Mi)chael (Frimyer, Michael)
Fuller, ... (Fuller, Jeremiah)
Funda, Jacob (Fonda, Jacob)
Funda, Jellis J. (Fonda, Jellis T£)
Gardner, William (Gardner, William)
Gibson, John (Gibson, John)
Glen, Isaac (Glen, Isaac)
Glover, Thomas (Glover, Thomas)
Gordon, ... (Gordon, Jonathan)
Groat, ... (Groat, Abraham C.)
Groat, Simon (Groat, Simon)
Gyberson, ... (Geberson, Daniel)
Hackney, George (Hackney, George)
Hagedorn, Harmanus (Hagedorn, Harmanes)
Hall, ... (Hall, Alexander)
```

Hall, Nicholas (Hall, Nicholas)
Hall, William (Hall, William)
Hallenbeck, ... (Hallenbeck, Michael)
Hallenbeek, ... (Hallenbeck, Michael)
Hanes, Jacobus (not in Fed. Census)
Harmens, ... (Harmann, Jacob)
Harnam, John (Haner, John)
Harton, ... (Hetherington, Elias)
Harton, ... (Hetherington, Sakley)
Heits, John (Hutton, John)
Herre, Samuel (Muray, Samuel)
Hewn, ... non est
Hooghtaling, James (Houghtalen, James)
Hoople, George (Hupple, George)
Hopkins, Joseph (Hopkins, Joseph)
Horsford, Peggy (Horseford, Margaret)
House, ... (House, John)
Humphrey, John (Humphrys, John)
Hunsicker, Frederick (Housicker, Frederick)
Ingeldson, Francis (Ingleston, Francis)
James, William (James, William)
Johnson, ... (Johnston, Edward)
Jones, (Sam)uel (Jones, Samuel)
Jones, ... (Jones, Samuel, Junr)
Joys, John (Joys, John)
Kelley, Alexander (Kelly, Alexander)
Kennedy, ... (Kennedy, James)
Kennedy, ... (Kennedy, John)
Kennedy, ..., Junr (Kennedy, John, Junr)
Kinsley, Joseph (Kinsley, Joseph)
Kittle, David (Kittle, David)
Kittle, Douw (Kittle, Down)
Labon, ... (Lebbin, John F.)
Lambert, John (Lambert, John)
Lewis, ...(Lewis, John)
(Lig)hthall, ... (Litehall, James)
Lighthall, Nicholas (Lighthall, Nicholas)
Linkwiser, Michael (Linkwiser, Michael)
McCemel, ...
McClennen, ... (McClennen, John)
McConnel, ... (McConnel, John)
McCoran, ...
McDougall, Duncan (McDougall, Duncan)
McEarly, John (McEarley, John)
McFarlen, Andrew (McFarlan, Andrew)
McFarlen, Malkum (McFarlan, Malcom)
McGage, ... (McGaghe, Samuel)
McGee, John (McGee, John)
McGregor, ... (McGrigger, Samuel)
McIntire, John (McIntire, John)
McIntosh, Anges (McIntosh, Angus)
McKue, ... (McKue, James)
McMarling, ... (McMullen, William)
McMikle, Alexander (McMickle, Alexander)

M^CMikle, Dirck
M^CMikle, James (M^CMickle, James)
M^CWilliams, ... (M^CWilliams, James)
Mabie, ... (Mabee, Hester)
Mane, William (Mayne, William)
Mannin, Christopher (Manning, Christopher)
Martin, ... (Martin, Charles)
Mercelis, John (Mersielus, John)
Mercelis, Mary (Marsielus, Mary)
Merselis, Helena (Merselis, Helena)
..., Chearls (Metier, Charles)
Milton, Charles (Miller, Charles)
Moore, John (Moore, John)
Moore, John (Murray, John)
Morrow, Alexander (Morrow, Alexander)
Morrow, James (Morrow, James)
Morston, ... (Mostin, Robert)
Mulmine, John (Mulmine, John)
Mynderse, Johannes (Minderse, John)
Nenling, Richard (Leaning, Richard)
Nieley, Matthew (Neely, Matthew)
Nisboth, ...h (Nesbitt, Joseph)
Obryn, ... (Obrien, Thomas)
Ogden, John (Ogden, John)
Ogden, John C. (Ogden, John)
Olsiver, ...bastian (Alsaver, Bastian)
Oosterhuyte, ... (not in Fed. Census)
Osborn, Francis (Osborn, Francis)
Ostrander, Hendrick (Ostrander, Hendrick)
Ostrander, Peter (Ostrander, Peter)
Ostrander, Peter (Ostrander, Peter)
(Os)trander, ... (Ostrander, Teunis)
Ostrander, William (Ostrander, William)
Ouderkerk, Arent (Onderkirk, Aaron)
Pankburn, Peter (not in Fed. Census)
Papson, Thomas (Pipson, Thomas)
Passage, George (Passage, George)
Patterson, Francis (Patterson, Francis)
Patterson, Thomas (Patterson, Thomas)
Paul, John (Paul, John)
Pauldon, John (Paulding, John)
Peak, ... (Peek, Henry)
Peek, Christopher (Peck, Christopher)
Peek, ... (Peek, Cornelius)
Peek, ... (Peek, Cornelius C.)
Peek (or Peck?), ... (Peek, Henry H.)
Peek (or Peck?), John (Peck, John J.)
Peek (or Peck?), Sarah (Peek, Sarah)
Perkens, ... (not in Fed. Census)
Peters, ... (Peters, Hermanus)
Peters, ..., Junr (Peters, Hermanus, Junr)
Peterson, Peter (Peterson, Peter)
Pickings, James (Pickins, James)
(P)rince, ... (Prince, John)

Putman, ... (Putman, Aaron)
Putman, Teunis (Putman, Tunis)
(Quac)kenboss, ...
Quackenboss, ... (Quackenbuss, Isaac)
Quackenboss, ... (Quackenbuss, Perardus)
Ratherford, Nelice (Rutherford, Nelies)
Renix, ... (Rannix, Andrew)
Rinix, John (Rennix, John)
Robertson, John (Robison, John)
Rogers, John (Rogers, John)
Rosa, ... (Rose, Mary)
Russell, ... (Russell, Benjamin)
Ryckman, ... (Ryckman, John)
Sacket, ... (Sacket, Jessee)
Sackman, Calvin (Pickman, Calvin)
Schermerhorn, ...
Schermerhorn, ... (Schermerhorn, Abraham)
Schermerhorn, ... (Schermerhorn, Barnardus T.)
Schermerhorn, Bartholomew (not in Fed. Census)
Schermerhorn, ... (Schermerhorn, Jacob)
Schermerhorn, Jacob (Schermerhorn, Jacob)
Schermerhorn, ... (Schermerhorn, John)
Schermerhorn, John (Schermerhorn, John)
Schermerhorn, ... (Schermerhorn, Ryer)
Schermerhorn, Ryer (Schermerhorn, Ryer)
Schermerhorn, Rykert (Schermerhorn, Rykert)
Schermerhorn, ... (Schermerhorn, Simon)
Schermerhorn, William (Schermerhorn, William)
Seager, Peter (Sager, Peter)
Shannan, John (Shannan, John)
Sharp, Matthias (Sharp, Matthias)
Shea, Nancy (Shee, Nancy)
Shelley, Samuel (Shelley, Samuel)
Shillen, ... (Shilling, Alexander)
(Shir)tliff, ... (Shirtliff, Joseph)
Shoemaker, John (Schonmaker, John)
Simmons, Reuben (Simons, Reuben)
Simson, ...
Sixby, (N)icholas (Saxbis, Nicholas)
Sluyter, ... (Slyter, Nicholas)
Smilie, John (Smiley, John)
Smith, ...
Smith, ...
Smith, Fanney (Smith, Fanny)
Smith, ... (Smith, John)
Snell, Major (Snell, Major)
Staley, ... (Staley, George)
Staley, Jacob (Staley, Jacob)
Stevens, Janetie (Stevens, Jannatie)
Stevens, Jonathan (Stevens, Jonathan)
Stevens, Mary (Stephens, Mary)
Stewart, ... (Stewart, John)
Stritzer, Christian (Slitser, Christian)

Stuart, James (Stewart, James)
Suypard, David (Luyphard, David)
Suypard, Jacob (Luyphard, Jacob)
Swart, ... (Swart, Jacob)
Swits, ... (Switz, Volkie)
Tanner, Robert (Tanning, Robert)
Taus, ... (Taws, David)
Taylor, Solomon (Taylor, Solomon)
Teller, Henry (Teller, Henry)
Teller, Mary (Teller, Mary)
Teller, ... (Teller, William)
(Tem)pleton, ... (Templeton, Thomas)
(Ten) Eyck, ... (Ten Eyck, Henry)
(Ten) Eyck, ... (Ten Eyck, Jacob)
(Ten) Eyck, ... (Ten Eyck, Mynderse S.)
Thompson, ... (Thompson, Alexander)
Thompson, William (Thompson, William)
Thornton, John (Thornton, John)
Toll, ... (Toll, David)
Toll, ... (Toll, John)
Tollhammer, Andrew (Tollhammer, Andrew)
Tonyhill, Robert (Tunnehill, Robert)
Truax, Andries (Truax, Andress)
Truax, ... (Truax, John)
Truax, Peter (Truax, Peter)
Van Alen, ... (Van Aulen, Peter)
Van Antwerp, ... (Van Antwerp, Abraham)
Van Antwerp, Arent (V:Antwerp, Arent)
Van Antwerp, Gerrit (Van Antwerp, Garrit)
Van Antwerp, Simon (Van Antwerp, Simon)
Van Benthysse, Martin (Van Beutheyson, Martin)
Van Cise, ... (Van Syce, Jacobus)
Van Debogert, Joseph (Van de Bogert, Joseph)
(Van Ue)bogert, ... (Van de Bogert, Nicholas)
Van Derheyden, David (Van der Hyden, David)
Vandevolgen, ... (Van der Volker, Rebecca)
Van Dyck, (Corne)lius (Van Dyke, Cornelius)
Van Dyck, Hendrick (Van Dyke, Hendrick)
Van Dyck, ... (Van Dyke, Henry)
Van Dyck, Peter (Van Dyke, Peter)
(Van) Dyck, ... (Van Dyck, Peter)
Van Eps, Jacobus (Van Eps, Jacobus)
Van Eps, Jacobus S. (V:Eps, Jacobus)
Van Eps, John (Van Eps, John)
Van Eps, ... B.J. (Van Eps, John Baptiste)
(Van) Eps (Van Eps, John Baptist)
Van Eps, John S. (V:Eps, John)
Van Eps, Sander (V:Eps, Sanders)
Van Etten, ... (not in Fed. Census)
Van Etten, Benjamin (not in Fed. Census except
                     in Rensselaerwick)
Van Etten, ... (not in Fed. Census)
(Van Ger)sling, ... (Van Gersling, Peter)
Van Guysling, Elias (Van Geysting, Elias)

Van Guysling, ... (Van Geysting, Jacob)
Van Houten, ... (Van Houten, Garrit)
(Van) Ingen, ... (Van Ingin, Dirick)
Van Patten, Andries (Van Patten, Anress)
Van Patten, Dirck (Van Patten, Dirck)
Van Patten, Nichololas (Van Patten, Nicholas)
Van Patten, ... (Van Patten, Nicholas)
Van Peek, ... (Peek, Cornelius C.)
Van Pelt, ... (Van Pelt, Peter)
Van Sandfoord, ... (Van Zanford, Cornelius)
Van Schaick, ... (Van Schaick, Garrit)
Van Sice, Simon (Van Sice, Simon)
(Van) Slyck, ... (Van Slyk, Adam)
Van Slyck, ... (Van Slyck, Anthony)
Van Slyck, Cornelius A. (Van Slyke, Cornelius A.)
Van Slyck, Harmanus (Van Slyke, Hermanus)
Van Slyck, ... (Van Slyke, Hermanus)
Van Slyck, Jesse (Van Slyke, Jesse)
Van Vorst, ... (Van Vorst, Jacobus)
Van Vorst, ... (Van Vorst, Jacobus J.)
Van Vorst, Jellis (V:Voorst, Zellis)
Van Vorst, ... (Van Vorst, Jellis J.)
Van Vorst, John B.T. (V:Vorst, John Baptist)
Van Vorst, John J. (V:Voorst, John S.)
Van Vranken, Harriantie (Van Vrankin, Ariancha)
Van Vranken, Maus (Van Vrankin, Maus)
Van Vranken, Nicholas (Van Vrankin, Nicholas)
Van Vranken, ... (Van Vrankin, Rykirt)
Van Wormer, Casper (not in Fed. Census)
Vedder, ... (Vedder, Aaron)
Vedder, ... A. (Vedder, Albert A.)
Vedder, Alexander (Veeder, Alexander)
Vedder, Arent S. (Veeder, Aaron S.)
Vedder, ... (Vedder, Francis)
Vedder, Harmen (Veeder, Harma)
Vedder, Harmen (Vedder, Hermanus)
Vedder, Philip (Vedder, Philip)
Veeder, Albert S. (Veeder, Albert S.)
Veeder, Catherine (Veeder, Catherine)
Veeder, ... (Veeder, Francis)
Veeder, Gerrit S. (Veeder, Garrit S.)
Veeder, Hendrick H. (Veeder, Hendrick H.)
Veeder, ... (Vedder, Immitie)
Veeder, Johannis (Veeder, John)
Veeder, John (Veeder, John)
Veeder, Nicholas (Veeder, Nicholas)
Veeder, Peter S. (Veeder, Peter S.)
Veeder, Simon (Vedder, Simon)
Veeder, ... (Veeder, Simon B.)
Veeder, ... (Veeder, Simon H.)
Velthuysen, ... (Veltheysen, Christopher)
Velthuysen, ... (Veltheuysen, Jacob)
Vielen, ... (Veelen, Nicholas)
Vrooman, Adam S. (Vrooman, Adam S.)

Vrooman, Alida (Vrosman, Aleda)
Vrooman, ... (Vrooman, Simon)
(W)aggener, ... (Waggoner, Emanuel)
Waggoner, George (Waggener, George)
Walker, Benjamin (Walker, Benjamin)
Watson, Alexander (Watson, Alexander)
Weaver, Hanikle (Weaver, Honicle)
Weeler, John (not in Fed. Census)
Weeler, Robert (not in Fed. Census)
Wells, ... (Williams, Frederick)
Wemley, ...
Wemple, ...
Wemple, John (Wemple, John)
Wemple, Myndert (Wemple, Myndert)
Wendell, Nancey Ellice (Ellis, Nancy)
Wendell, Robert H. (Wendell, Robert H.)
Wesselse, ... (Wessells, Herman)
Wesselse, ... (Wessells, Mary)
Wheaton, Reuben (Weaton, Reuben)
Wheaton, Thomas (Weaton, Thomas)
Whiley, ... (Wilkie, Thomas)
White, ... (White, Benjamin)
White, Peter (White, Peter)
White, William (White, William)
(Wi)lliamson, ...
Willis, ... (Willis, John)
(W?)ynderse, ... (Wynderse, Jacobus)
Yates, Jane (Yates, Jane)
Yates, Joseph R. (Yates, Joseph R.)
Yates, Nicholas (Yates, Nicholas)
Yates, ... (Yates, Yellis)
Young, Benjamin (Young, Benjamin)
Young, Calvin (Young, Calvin)

SCHOHARIE
Anthony, Albert[S] (Anthony, Albertus)
Anthony, Jacob (Anthony, Jacob)
Backer, Jn[o] C. (Becker, John C.)
Backer, Nicholas (Becker, Nicholas)
Ball, Peter (Ball, Peter)
Barner, George (Barner, George)
Barner, Joseph (Barner, Joseph)
Barnes, Isaac (Barns, Isaac)
Barnes, Johann[S] (Barner, Johannes)
Barnhayt, ... (Bernard, Hermanus)
Becker, David (Becker, David)
Becker, Joh[S] H. (Becker, Johannes H.)
Becker, Joh[S] J. (Becker, Johannes J£)
Becraft, W[m] (Becraft, William)
Bellinger, Joh[S] (Bellinger, Johannes)
Bellinger, Joseph (Bellinger, Yost)
Bellinger, Marc[S] (Bellinger, Marcus)
Berger, Wilhelm[S] (Berger, Wilhelmus)
Bergh, Phillip (Bergh, Philip)

Bont, Peter (Bont, Peter)
Borst, (Johannes) J. (Borst, Johannes J.)
Borst, Peter (Borst, Peter)
Bost, Hend^k (Borst, Henry)
Bouck, ... (Bouck, Christian)
Bouck, Corn^s (Bouck, Cornelius)
Bouck, ... (Bouck, Johannes)
Bouck, Lourence (Bouck, Lawrence)
Bouck, Nich^s (Bouck, Nicholas)
Bouck, Thom^s (Bouck, Yhomas)
Bouck, W^m (Bouck, William)
Bouck, ... (Bouck, William)
Brown, ...
Brown, ... (Brown, Adam)
Brussell, Johan S. (not in Fed. Census)
Budd, Daniel (Budd, Daniel)
Cater, (Adam) (Keater, Adam)
Curtice, Danl (Curtis, Daniel)
Deo, David (Deo, David)
Dietz, W^m (Dietz, William)
Domnick, Jno (Dominick, John)
Ecker, W^m (Ecker, William)
Ecker, ... (Ecker, Yost)
Eggleman, Hendrick (Engleman, Hendrick)
Enders, ... (Enders, Jacob)
Enders, ..., Junr (Enders, John, Junr)
Enders, Peter, Junr (Enders, Peter, Junr)
Enders, W^m (Enders, William)
Enselt, ... (Enfield, Bastian)
Feck, (Jac)ob (Feck, Jacob)
Feck, Johann^s (Feck, Johannes)
Fink, W^m (Fink, William)
Fryinger, ... (Frimyer, Conradt)
Gauss, Jno (Gass, John)
Goodwin, Solom^n (Goodwin, Solomon)
Heager, Hendrick (Heager, Hendrick)
Heager, ... (Heager, Johannes)
Heager, ..., Junr (Heager, Johannes, Junr)
Hibsman, Hendrick (Hidsman, Henry)
Hills, George (Hills, George)
(Hit?)siner, ... (Hitsiner, Michael)
(Hit?)sman, ... (Hitsman, John)
Houck, ...
Houck, Hendrick (Houck, Henry)
House, Henry (House, Henry)
Hunton, Joseph (Hunton, Joseph)
Keller, Adam (Keller, Adam)
Keyser, ... (Keyser, Johannes)
King, (Leonar)d (King, Leonard)
King, (Mich)ael (King, Michael)
Kinney, Dydemus (Kenny, Dydemus)
Kneuskern, Jno (Keniskern, John)
Kneuskern, Jost (Keniskern, Jost)
Knieskern, ...

Kyser, Andrew [Keyser, Andrew]
Larns, ...
Lawyer, Johannis [Lawyer, Johannes]
Lawyer, Joh^s L. [Lawyer, Johannes L.]
Lawyer, Lourence [Lawyer, Lawrence]
Lee, Jonath^n [Lee, Jonathan]
Loop, Andrew [Loop, Andrew]
Loucks, And^r [Louks, Andrew]
Loucks, ... [Louks, William]
Lovegay, Obad. [Lovejoy, Obediah]
McKinzie, ...
Mann, Jacob [Mann, Jacob]
Mann, ... [Mann, Peter]
Matthias, Adam [Matice, Adam]
Matthias, Fred^k [Matice, Frederick]
Matthias, Yost [Matice, Yost]
Mattias, Conradt [Matice, Conradt]
Mattias, Hendrick [Matice, Hendrick, Junr]
Mattias, Niecholas [Matice, Nicholas]
Mattias, Johan^s, Junr [Matice, Johannes, Junr]
Mellon, Henry [Mellon, Henry]
Merkle, [Hendr]ick [Merckle, Henry]
Myers, ... [Myers, Christopher]
Myers, ... [Myers, Jacob]
Myers, ... [Myers, Stephen]
Otto, Vroman [not in Fed. Census]
Peck, Marti^s [Peck, Martinus]
Plouck, ... [Plounck, Hendrick]
Poole, Jester [Pool, Jester]
Richardson, ... [Richardson, William]
Rightmyer, George [Rightmyer, George]
Rorick, Casper [Rorick, Casper]
Ruck, ... [Rusk, John]
Rusue, Jno [Rusue, John]
Rykert, Geo. [Rykert, George]
Rykert, Johannes [Rickart, Johannes]
Rykert, ... [Rickart, Nicholas]
Schoolcraft, Jacob [Schoolcraft, Jacob]
Schoolcraft, Johann^s [Schoolcraft, Honest]
Schoolcraft, Lawrence [Schoolcraft, Lawrence]
Seeley, Martinus [Sealey, Martinus]
Seeley, Peter [Sealey, Peter]
Seksberger, Jacob [Saltsberger, Jacob]
Shafer, ...
Shaver, Marcus [Shaffer, Marcus]
Shell, Jacob F. [Shell, Jacob F.]
Shell, Jost [Shell, Jost]
Simmer, Adam [Zimmer, Adam]
Simmer, Peter [Zimmer, Peter]
Simmer, W^m [Simmer, William]
Skillman, ... [Shillman, George]
Sloth, Henry [Sloth, Henry]
Smith, Christ^r [Smith, Christian]
Snyder, ...

Snyder, ...
Snyder, ..., Jun[r]
Snyder, George (Snyder, George)
Snyder, Johann[s] (Snyder, Johannes)
Snyder, Peter (Snyder, Peter)
Sperry, Aaron (Perry, Aaron)
Staats, Thomas (Statts, Thomas)
Stall, Letteen (Stoll, Latham)
Sternberger, ... (Strubergh, Lambert)
Steenbergh, ...
Sternbergh, Abrah[m] (Sternbergh, Abraham)
Sternbergh, David (Sternbergh, David)
Sternbergh, Jacob (Sternbergh, Jacob)
Sternbergh, Nichols (Sternburgh, Nicholas)
Stewart, Henry (Stewart, Henry)
Swart, Bart[w] (Swart, Bartholomew)
Swart, Laurence (Swart, Lawrence)
Swart, Teunisse (Swart, Teunis)
Tuffs, W[m] (Tuffs, William)
Van Allen, ... (Van Autin, Philip)
Van Dyke, Cornel[s] (Van Dyke, Cornelius)
Van Slyke, Martinus (Van Slyke, Martinus)
Volkenbergh, Herman (Van Volkinburgh, Herman)
Volkinbergh, ... (Van Volkinburgh, Jost)
Visher, W[m] (Visscher, William)
Vroman, ...
Vroman, Adam (Vrooman, Adam)
Vroman, Adam B. (Vrooman, Adam B.)
Vroman, Bar[t] (Vrooman, Barent)
Vroman, Bart[w] (Vrooman, Bartholomew C.)
Vroman, Ephraim (Vroman, Ephraim)
Vroman, Jn[o], Jun[r] (Vrooman, John, Jun[r])
Vroman, Jonas (Vroman, Jonas)
Vroman, Peter A. (Vrooman, Peter A.)
Vroman, Peter C. (Vrooman, Peter C.)
Vroman, ... J. (Vrooman, Peter J.)
Vroman, Sam[l] (Vroman, Samuel)
Wadwell, David (Wardell, David)
Ward, (Ze)dick (Ward, Zedick)
Warner, ... (Warner, Jost)
Witney, ... (Witney, John)
Woodruff, Charles (Woodruff, Charles)
Worth, Johan[s] (Worth, Johannes)
Yamson, Johann[s] (Yanson, Johannes)
Yanson, Hendrick (Yanson, Hendrick)
Youngs, Jacob (Youngs, Jacob)
Zeeraft, (Jaco)b (Zeacraft, Jacob)
Zeu, Jost (Zeh, Jost)

STEPHENTOWN
Able, Aaron (Abbe, Aaron)
Adams, ... (Adams, James)
Adams, ..., Jun[r] (Adams, James, Ju[r])
Allen, ... (Allen, James)

Allen, John (Allen, John)
Allen, ... (Allen, Stephen)
Alsworth, John (Elsworth, John)
(Al)sworth, ... (Elsworth, Josiah)
Andres, Solomon (Andrews, Solomon)
(A)ndrew, ... (Andrews, Holden)
Andros, Samuel (Andrews, Samuel)
Armstrong, Samuel (Armstrong, Samuel)
Arnold, Eleazer (Arnold, Eleezer)
Arnold, (S)tephen (Arnold, Stephen)
Astin, ... (Asplin, Samuel)
Austin, Isaac (Austin, Isaac)
Babcock, Amos (Babcock, Amos)
Babcock, Amos, Junr (Babcock, Amos, Jur)
(Ba)bcock, ... (Babcock, Enoch)
Babcock, Hezeriah (Babcock, Ezariah)
Babcock, ... (Babcock, John B.)
Babcock, Newman (Babcock, Newman)
Babins, John (Babins, John)
Bailey, Ameziah (Bailey, Amasia)
Bailey, Widow (Bailey, Ann)
Baken, ...
Baker, Joseph (Baker, Joseph)
Baker, (Rey)nolds (Baker, Renolds)
Baldwin, Nathan (Baldwin, Nathan)
Baldwin, Nathan W. (Baldwin, Nathan W.)
Baley, Stanton (Bailey, Stanten)
Baley, Thomas (Bailey, Thomas)
Baley, Thomas, Junr (Bailey, Thomas, Jr)
Barber, Edward (Barber, Edward)
Barber, Ezeriah (Barber, Ezariah)
Barber, Noome (Barber, Naoma)
Barney, ... (Burris, Charles)
Barrey, ... (Barry, Elisha)
Barrey, ..., Jr (Barry, Elisha, Jr)
Bartlet, ... (Bartlet, John)
Bass, ... (Bliss, Abisha)
Bateman, ... (Bateman, Ruben)
Bates, Joseph (Bates, Joseph)
Batey, Elijah (Bailey, Elisha)
Bayley, Timothy (Bailey, Timothy)
Beckwith, ... (Beckwith, Charles)
Benjamin, Ebenezer (Benjamin, Ebenezer)
Bennet, Ephraim (Bennet, Ephraim)
Bennet, Ezra (Bennet, Ezra)
Bennet, Israel (Bennet, Israel)
Bennet, ... (Bennet, Jesse)
(Be)nnet, ... (Bennett, John)
Bennet, Nathaniel (Bennett, Nathl)
Bennet, ... (Bennett, Willm)
Bentley, ... (Bentley, Benjn)
Bentley, ... (Bentley, Caleb)
Bentley, Eldrid (Bentley, Eldrid)
Bentley, John (Bentley, John)

Bentley, John, J^r (Bentley, John, J^r)
Bentley, Joshua (Bently, Joshua)
Bentley, ... (Bentley, Oliver)
(Be)ntley, ..., J^r (Bently, Oliver, Ju^r)
Bentley, Reuben (Bentley, Ruben)
Bentley, Thomas (Bentley, Thomas)
Berrey, ... (Berry, Charles)
Billing, ... (Billings, Ebenezer)
Blake, Freelove (Blake, Freelove)
Bloss, John (Bliss, John)
Bloss, ... (Bliss, Menessah)
Bly, Clark (Bly, Clerk)
Bly, Jonathan (Bly, Jonathan)
Bonesteel, ... (Bonestate, Henry)
Bosell, ... (Bosell, James)
Boughten, Jonathan (Boughton, Jonathan)
Boughten, William (Boughton, Willm)
Bourman, William (Boorman, Willm)
Bowen, ... (Bowers, Stephen)
Bozworth, ... (Bosworth, Hezekiah)
Braman, ... (Brannum, Paul)
Bramon, Rebeca (Breman, Rebecka)
Brand, ... (Brend, David)
Braton, Gideon (Braton, Gideon)
Braton, Gideon, Junr (Braton, Gideon, Ju^r)
Braton, ... (Braton, Thomas)
Breyf, ... (Briggs, Zephanieh)
Briggs, ... (Briggs, Cristopher)
Briggs, Ezeriah (Briggs, Ezariah)
Briggs, Job (Briggs, Job)
Briggs, John (Briggs, John)
Briggs, ... (Briggs, Thomas)
Brimer, Godfrey (Brimmer, Godfrey)
Brimer, Jacob (Brimmer, Jacob)
Brimer, John, Junr (Brimmer, John, Ju^r)
Brimmer, John (Brimmer, John)
Brockway, Reed (Brockaway, Reed)
Brockway, ... (Brockaway, Silence)
Brookins, ... (Brookins, Ephraim)
Brookins, ..., J^r (Brookins, Ephraim, J^r)
Brown, Alexander (Brown, Alex^r)
Brown, ..., Junr (Brown, Caleb, Ju^r)
Brown, ... (Brown, Daniel)
Brown, John (Brown, John)
Brown, Jonathan (Brown Jonathan)
Brown, Jonathan (Brown, Jonathan)
Brown, Naboth (Brown, Nabath)
Brown, Nehemiah (Brown, Nehemiah)
Brown, Noah (Brown, Noah)
Brown, ... (Brown, Peter)
Brown, Robert (Brown, Robert)
Brown, Samuel (Brown, Samuel)
Brown, ... (Brown, Solomon)
Brown, Timothy (Brown, Timothy)

Brown, William (Brown, Willm)
Brown, Zebulon (Brown, Zebulon)
Burdick, Cary, Junr (Burdick, Carey, Junr)
Burdick, ... (Burdih, Daniel)
Burdick, Fillamus (Burdick, Zillemas)
Burdick, ... (Burdick, Jabez)
Burdick, ... (Burdick, Zacheus)
Burdock, Cary (Burdick, Cary)
Burtch, Gideon (Burtch, Gideon)
Burtch, Jacob (Burtch, Jacob)
Bush, Capt Abijah (Bush, Abijah)
Bush, Moses (Bush, Moses)
Cady, ... (Cady, Isaac)
Cady, ... (Cady, Lois)
Cammel, (Jo)hn (Campbell, John)
Cummins, Jacob (Cummins, Jacob)
Cane, John (Coon, John)
(Carp)ender, ... (Carpenter, Samuel)
(Carp)ender, ... (Carpenter, Thomas)
Carpenter, Joseph (Carpenter, Joseph)
(Ca)rpenter, ... (Carpenter, Willm)
Carpenter, William (Carpenter Willm)
Carr, ... (Carr, Edward)
Carr, ... (Carr, Joseph)
Carr, Richmond (Kerr, Richmond)
Carr, ... (Kerr, Stafford)
Carr, ... (Kerr, Thurston)
Carrice, Amaziah (Convis, Amenia)
Casy, ... (Casey, Adam)
Casey, Jessey (Casey, Jesse)
Caton, ... (Eaton, Lott)
Chace, ... (Chase, Consider)
Champlain, Michael (Champlin, Michael)
Chapman, Caleb (Chapman, Caleb)
Chard, Stephen (Ord, Stephen)
Chase, Henry (Chace, Henry)
Chase, ... (Chace, Tolman)
Chatsey, Joseph (Chetsey, Joseph)
Church, Jonathan (Church, Jonathan)
Clark, Carey (Clerk, Corey)
Clark, Elisha (Clerk, Elisha)
Clark, Gideon (Clerk, Gardner)
Clark, John (Clerk, John)
Clark, John, Junr (Clerk, John, Ju^r)
Clark, ... (Clerk, Joseph)
Clark, ... (Clerk, Samuel)
Clark, ... (Clerk, Thomas)
Clear, ... (Clear, Joseph)
Coats, Christopher (Colts, Christopher)
Coats, Daniel (Oats, Daniel)
Cohoen, Nathaniel (Cahoon, Nathl)
Cole, Aaron (Cole, Amos)
Cole, William (Cole, Willm)
Cole, Zepheniah (Cole, Zepheniah)

(Col)egrove, ... (Colegrove, Samuel)
Colegrow, Christopher (Colegrove, Christopher)
Colwell, ... (Caldwell, Thomas)
Cone, Elemanden (Cone, Elmmdin)
Cook, ... (Cook, Abiel)
Cook, Joseph (Cook, Joseph)
Cook, Lambert (Cook, Lanabert)
Cook, Levy (Cook, Levi)
Coon, Hezekiah (Coon, Hezekiah)
Coon, Hezekiah, Junr (Coon, Hezekiah, Ju^r)
Coon, Jamas (Coon, James)
Coon, John (Coon, John)
Coon, Jonathan (Coon, Jonathan)
Coon, Nathan (Coon, Nathan)
Coon, Prentis (Coon, Prentiss)
Coon, William (Coon, William)
(Co)pwell, ... (Copwell, Willm)
Corey, ... (Cray, John G.)
Cottonal, Libus (Catterel, Lebeus)
Cowdre, David (Cowder, David)
Crandall, Jeremiah (Crandell, Jeremiah)
Crandall, John (Crandell, John)
(Cr)andall, ... (Crandell, John)
Crandall, Laban (Crandell, Laban)
Crandall, Mary (Crandell, Mary)
Crandall, ... (Crandell, Ransel)
Crandall, ... (Crandell, Samuel)
Crandall, William (Crandell, Willm)
Crandol, Stephen (Crandell, Stephen)
Cranston, John (Cranstin, John)
Crapsie, ... (Cropsin, Jacob)
Crapsie, ... (Cropsin, John C.)
Critter, Robert (Critler, Robert)
Cronkright, ... (Cronkright, John)
Cronkright, ... (Cronkright, Simon)
Crork, William (Clerk, Willm)
(Cr)umb, ... (Crumb, Wait S.)
Crumb, ... (Crumb, Willm)
Cummins, Etheel (Cummins, Ethul)
Curtis, James (Custis, James)
Curtis, ... (Custis, Joel)
Curtis, Thomas (Curtin, Thomas)
Curtis, Thomas, J^r (Custis, Thomas, Ju^r)
Darror, Emores (Darrow, Emosas)
Davids, David (Davis, David)
(D)avis, ... (Davis, George)
Davis, ... (Davis, Willm)
Davis, ... (Davis, Willm)
Day, Anna (Day, Anna)
Day, Stephen (Day, Stephen)
Deemer, Elisha (Divener, Elisha)
Delano, Reuben (Delano, Ruben)
Denison, Charles (Dennim, Charles)
(De)niston, ... (Dennison, Daniel)

Deniston, ... (Dennison, Jonathan)
Dent, ... (Dent, Nathan)
Deverix, Elisha (Deverix, Elisha)
Dixson, John (Dixon, John)
Dolley, ... (Dolley, Isaac)
Doosenbury, Gabriel (Dosenberry, Gabriel)
Doty, Joseph (Doty, Joseph)
Doty, William (Doty, Willm)
Douglass, ... (Douglass, Willm)
Dudley, ... (Dudley, Freeman)
Duglass, ... (Douglass, Asa)
Dunum, ... (Dunnam, Isaac)
(Du)senbury, ... (Dusenberry, Henry)
Dyman, Isaac (Diamon, Isaac)
Eady, ... (Eady, Asaph)
Edwards, Henry (Edwards, Henry)
Elabert, John (Elabert, John)
Eldred, ... (Eldridge, Willm)
Eldredge, Samuel (Eldridge, Samuel)
Eles, J(a)cob (Ellis, Jacob)
Emerson, Mary (Emmerson, Mary)
Emmons, ... (Emerson, Jonathan)
Evest, Amos (Evitts, Amos)
Ewins, John (Gravins, John)
Fall, John (Fall, John)
Fannin, ... (Fonnin, Jeremiah)
Fannin, ... (Fonnin, Willm)
Farce, David (Vorce, David)
Ferris, Ezra (Ferris, Ezra)
Finch, ... (Finch, Lewis)
Fitch, ... (Fitch, Prentis)
Fowler, Caleb (Fowler, Caleb)
Fox, ... (Fox, Martha)
Frasier, William (Frazier, Willm)
French, Sintha (not in Fed. Census)
Frisk, William (Fish, Willm)
Fuller, Amos (Fuller, Amos)
Fuller, Daniel (Fuller, Daniel)
Fuller, Jeduthan (Fuller, Jiduthen)
Gales, Jacob (Gates, Jacob)
Galleway, Joseph (Galloway, Joseph)
Gallop, ... (Galop, Rufus)
Galusha, Jacob (Galusha, Jacob)
Gardiner, ... (Gardiner, Anth^l)
Gardner, Henry (Gardiner, Henry)
Gardner, Oliver (Gardiner, Oliver)
Gardner, ... (Gardiner, Rowland)
Gates, Isaac (Gates, Isaac)
Gillet, ... (Gillet, Nathan)
(Gi)tto, ... (Gitto, Francis)
Godfrey, Benjamin (Godfrey, Benjn)
Godfrey, John (Godfrey, John)
Goodrich, Jeremiah (Goodrich, Jeremiah)
Goodrich, Jesse (Goodrich, Jesse)

Goodrich, Samuel (Goodrich, Samuel)
Graves, Ezra (Graves, Ezra)
Gray, Daniel (Grey, Daniel)
Green, Benjamin (Green, Benjn)
Green, ... (Green, Benjn)
Green, Caleb (Green, Caleb)
Green, Charles (Green, Charles)
Green, Jacob (Green, Jacob)
Green, Jeremiah (Green, Jeremiah)
Green, John (Green, John)
Green, Jonathan (Green, Jonathan)
Green, Joseph (Green, Joseph)
Green, Langford (Green, Langford)
Green, Luke (Green, Luke)
Green, Natha (Green, Nathan)
Green, Pery (Green, Perry)
Greenfield, Archabald (Greenfield, Archibald)
Greenfield, ... (Greenfield, Raymond)
Greenman, Nathan (Grinman, Nathan)
(Gr)eenman, ... (Greenman, Ruth)
Grey, John (Grey, John)
Griffeth, ... (Griffin, Jeremiah)
Griffeth, Nathan (Griffin, Nath^n)
Griffith, Abnor (Griffith, Abner)
Grinman, Benjamin (Grinman, Benjn)
Grinman, Sylvenus (Grinman, Silvanus)
(Gr)iswold, ... (Griswold, Menos)
Hais, Pheny (Hays, Pleny)
Hakes, Nathan (Hakes, Nathan)
Hall, ... (Hall, Benjn)
Hall, ... (Hale, Bredwick)
Hall, Christopher (Hale, Christopher)
Hall, ... (Hale, Isaac)
Hall, John (Hall, John)
Hall, Joshua (Hale, Joshua)
Hall, Oliver (Hall, Oliver)
Hall, ... (Hale, Rowland)
Hall, ... (Hall, Willm)
Hammon, Pardon (Hammond, Pardon)
Hammon, Stephen (Hammond, Stephen)
Hammond, John (Hammond, John)
Hanks, Benjamin (Hanks, Benjn)
Hard, ... (Hord, Nathan)
Harris, ... (Harris, Joseph)
Harris, (Nic)holas (Harris, Nicholas)
Harris, ..., Junr (Harris, Robert, J^r)
Hartshorn, William (Hartshorn, Willm)
Hempstead, Nathaniel (Hampsted, Nathl)
Hempsted, Thomas (Hampsted, Thomas)
Hendrick, Moses (Hendrik, Moses)
Herrington, ... (Henington, Isaac)
Herrington, ... (Herrington, Samuel)
(Herr)ington, ..., J^r (Herrington, Samuel)
Herington, Weightman (Herrington, Whitman)

Herrington, William (Herrington, Willm)
Herrick, ... (Herrik, Lebeus)
Hewit, ... (Hewitt, Jeptha)
Hill, Ebenezer (Hill, Ebenezer)
Hill, ... (Hill, Ebenezer)
Hill, Ebenezer, J^r (Hill, Ebenezer, Ju^r)
Hill, Thomas (Hill, Thomas)
Hill, William (Hill, Willm)
Hinckley, ... (Hinkley, Paul)
Hinds, ... (Hinds, Ruben)
Hinkley, ... (Hinkley, Samuel)
Hitchcox, William, Junr (Hitchcock, Willm, Ju^r)
Hoard, ... (Hoard, David)
Hoard, ... (Hoard, Edward)
Hoard, ... (Hoard, George)
Hoard, ... (Hoard, Simon)
Hogeboom, Jacob (Hageboom, Jacob)
Hogen, ... (Hagens, Simon)
Hogle, John (Hogel, John)
Holcomb, ... (Holcomb, Berich)
Holcomb, ... (Holcomb, Josiah)
Holmes, ...am (Holmes, Abraham)
Hoyd, Josiah (Hoyt, Josiah)
Huet, Samuel (Hurt, Samuel)
Huns, David (Harris, David)
Hunt, ... (Hunt, Aaren)
Hunt, ... (Hunt, Ruben)
Hunt, Ziba (Hunt, Zeba)
Huntington, Ezekiah (Huntington, Ezekiel)
Huntington, ... (Huntington, Ezekiel)
Hustus, David (Hurtis, David)
Inginbotham, Niles (Higginbottom, Niles)
Inman, ... (Inman, Nathan)
Irish, John (Irish, John)
Jackson, ... (Jackson, Ephraim)
James, Amos (James, Amos)
Jerona, Augustus (Jerom, Augustus)
Joles, Ebenezer (Joles, Ebenezer)
Joles, ... (Joles, Jeremiah)
Jones, Henry (Jones, Henry)
Jones, James (Jones, James)
Kendel, David (Kendall, David)
Kendel, William (Kendall, William)
Kinyon, William (Kenyon, Willm)
Kittle, Edmon (Kittle, Edmond)
Kittle, Ephraim (Kittle, Ephraim)
Kittle, ... (Kittle, Willm)
(K)ittle, ... (Kittle, Willm)
Knap, Biell (Nap, Beil)
Knap, ...ben, Junr (Knap, Ruben, J^r)
Knolton, Joseph (Knotten, Joseph)
(Lam)phier, ... (Lamphier, Amos)
Lamphier, Isaiah (Lamphear, Isaiah)
Lamphier, ... (Lamphear, Solomon)

Lamphire, Abraham (Lamphear, Abraham)
Lamphire, ... (Lamphear, Nimrod)
(L)ampman, ... (Lentman, Henry)
Lampman, Jacob (Lentman, Jacob)
Lampman, John (Lentman, John)
Landers, ... (Lendirs, Caleb)
Laraba, ... (Larabie, Theophilus)
Laraway, Philip (Laraway, Philip)
Latcher, John (Litcher, John)
Lawrance, Isaiah (Lawrence, Isaiah)
Leabernworth, ... (Lavensworth, David)
Lee, ... (Lee, Nenj^n)
Leetson, ... (Letson, Willm)
Letcher, Cornelius (Litcher, Cornelius)
Letcher, Hendrick (Litcher, Hendrick)
Letron, Robert (Letson, Robert)
Lewis, David (Lews, David)
(L)ewis, ... (Lewis, Elijah)
Lewis, James (Lewis, James)
Lewis, ... (Lewis, Joseph)
Lewis, Nehemiah (Lewis, Nehemiah)
Lewis, Zebulon (Lewis, Zebulon)
(Li)ttlefield, ... (Littlefield, Samuel)
Lobdell, Abijah (Lebdell, Abijah)
Lobdell, Jacob (Labdell, Jacob)
Lodington, ... (Laddington, Solomon)
Lundin, ... (London, Jeremiah)
McCarty, ... (McCarty, Daniel)
Maccumber, William (Macomber, Willm)
McKey, ... (McCoy, Silvester)
McPoe, John (Monroe, John)
McWain, Andrew (McWain, Andrew)
Main, ... (Main, Gilbert)
Main, ... (Main, James)
Main, Jeremiah (Main, Jeremiah)
Main, Jeremiah, Junr (Main, Jeremiah, Ju^r)
Main, Lothrop (Main, Lotrop)
Main, Nathan (Main, Nathan)
Main, William (Main, Willm)
Manchester, William (Manchester, Willm)
Mannem, (Augus)tus (Mannin, Augustus)
Mannin, Stephen (Mannin, Stephen)
Marks, ... (Marks, Hezekiah)
Marsel, ... (Marshall, Nathl)
Marton, ... (Morton, Elizer)
Marvin, ... (Marvin, John)
Matersons, Job (Mattison, Job)
Matteson, David (Mattison, David)
Maxson, Jered (Moxen, Jared)
Maxson, ... (Moxen, Stephen)
Mead, ... (Mead, Ezekiel)
Millard, Benjamin (Millard, Benjn)
Millard, John (Millard, John)
Moffitt, Hosea (Moffitt, Hosea)

Moon, Anna (Moon, Anna)
Moon, ... (Moore, Benoni)
Moon, Job (Moon, Job)
Moon, John (Moore, John)
Moon, John R. (Moon, John R.)
Moon, Micajah (Moon, Minjah)
Morey, William (Morey, Willm)
Morgin, John (Morgan, John)
Morton, Elisha (Martin, Elisha)
Mosher, Gabriel (Mosher, Gabriel)
Mosure, Hugh (Mosher, Hugh)
Mosure, Jonathan (Mosher, Jonathan)
Mote, Benjamin (Wiatt, Benjn)
Mott, ... (Mott, Ebenezer)
Murfee, John (Murphy, John)
Murray, ... (Murray, Alex^r)
Newbury, Simeon (Newberry, Simon)
Newcom, James (Newcomb, James)
Nicholds, Caleb (Nichols, Caleb)
Nicholds, David (Nichols, David)
Nicholds, John (Nichols, John)
Nicholds, Obadiah (Nichols, Obadiah)
Nicholds, Thomas (Nichols, Thomas)
Nichols, ... (Nichols, John)
Nichols, Jonathan (Nichols, Jonathan)
Nichols, ... (Nichols, Willm)
Niles, ... (Niles, Jonathan)
Niles, Samuel (Niles, Samuel)
Nills, ... (Niles, Stephen)
Northorp, Needham (Nortrup, Needham)
Northorp, Nicholas (Nortrup, Nicholas)
Northorp, Thomas (Nortrup, Thomas)
Northorp. Thomas (Nortrup, Thomas, J^r)
Northrep, Emanuel (Nortrup, Emanuel)
Oakley, Stephen (O'Mely, Stephen)
Odall, William (Odli, Willm)
Odell, Josep (Odle, Joseph)
Odle, Simeon (Odle, Simon)
Page, Winslow (Page, Winslow)
Pain, Simon (Pain, Simon)
Palmer, ... (Palmer, Joshua)
Palmer, ... (Palmer, Thomas)
Pardee, ... (Parden, Calvin)
Parmer, ... (Palmer, Ichabod)
Parr, ... (Parr, Moses)
Pattridge, Zackaiah (Potridge, Zachariah)
Philips, ...ham (Phillips, Abraham)
Philips, ... (Phillips, Ezekiel)
Philips, Isaac (Phillips, Isaac)
Philips, John (Phillips, John)
Philips, John, Junr (Phillips, John, Ju^r)
Philips, Peter (Phillips, Peter)
Philips, Thomas (Phillips, Thomas)
Pierce, ... (Pierce, Azuruim)

Pierce, David (Pierce, David)
Plate, Peter (Plate, Peter)
Plumb, ... (Plum, Henry)
Potter, Godfrey (Potter, Godfrey)
Potter, ... (Patton, Rowland)
Potter, ... (Pottor, Stephen)
Pratt, Zadock (Pratt, Zodock)
Proser, Abegail (Prosser, Abigal)
Proser, Ichabod (Prossar, Ichabod)
Proser, Jonathan (Prosser, Jonathan)
Quimbey, Ephraim (Quimbey, Ephraim)
Quimbey, James (Quimbey, James)
Randall, ... (Randall, Charles)
Randall, ... (Randall, David)
Randall, ... (Randall, Ichabod)
Randall, Jonathan (Randall, Jonathan)
Randall, ... (Randall, Joshua)
Randell, ... (Randall, Matthew)
Reynolds, ... (Renolds, Caleb)
Reynolds, Henry (Reynolds, Henry)
(Re)ynolds, ... (Reynolds, Joseph)
Reynolds, ... (Reynolds, Moses)
Reynolds, Simeon (Reynolds, Simon)
Rhodes, Abel (Rhodes, Abel)
Richard, James (Richards, James)
Ricker, Kellyhorn (Ricker, Kellyhorn)
Risenbareck, Henry (Risenbergh, Henry)
Robenson, ... (Robison, Ezra)
Robenson, ... (Robison, Jabez)
Robenson, Jeremiah (Robison, Jeremiah)
Robenson, Wheaten (Robinson, Wheaten)
Roberts, ... (Roberts, Benjn)
Roberts, Peter (Roberts, Peter)
Robinson, Ezra (Robison, Ezra)
Rodes, ... (Rhodes, Samuel)
Rogers, Joseph (Rogers, Joseph)
Rogers, Joseph (Rogers, Joseph)
Rogers, Joseph, Junr (Rogers, Joseph, Ju^r)
Root, Solomon (Root, Solomon)
Rose, ... (Rose, Wait)
Ross, Edward (Ross, Edward)
Rounds, ... (Rounds, Joseph)
Rounds, ..., Junr (Rounds, Joseph, J^r)
Rounds, ... (Rounds, Moses)
Rowlee, David (Rowley, David)
Rowlee, Reuben (Rowley, Ruben)
Rowlee, Timothy, Junr (Rowley, Timothy, J^r)
Rowley, Joseph (Rowley, Joseph)
Rowley, Nathaniel (Rowley, Nathl)
Russell, William (Russel, Willm)
Sabons, Joshua (Sabins, Joshua)
Sackett, John (Sacket, John)
Satterly, William (Satterly, William)
Satterly, William, J^r (Satterly, William, J^r)

Scrivens, ... (Scrivens, Joshua)
Scrivens, ... (Scrivens, Willm)
Scrivens, ... (Scrivens, Zebulon)
(Se)dgewick, ... (Sedgewick, Titus)
Semon, ... (Simmons, Jacob)
Semon, ... (Simmons, Jones)
Semon, ... (Simmons, Peter)
Semons, ... (Simmons, Jeremiah)
Sewell, Nicholas (Sewell, Nicholas)
Shaw, ... (Shaw, Anthony)
Shaw, ..., J^r (Shaw, Comfort, J^r)
Shaw, Samuel (Shaw, Samuel)
Shaw, Sarah (Shaw, Sarah)
Shelden, ... (Sheldon, Benjn)
Shelden, ... (Sheldon, Benjn)
(Sh)elden, ... (Sheldon, Ezekiel)
(She)lden, ... (Sheldon, Joseph)
(Sh)elden, ... (Sheldon, Ruth)
Shelden, ... (Sheldon, Stephen)
Shelden, William (Sheldon, Willm)
Sherman, Christopher (Sherman, Christopher)
Sherman, ... (Sherman, Peleg)
Sherman, Thomas (Sherman, Thomas)
(Sille)brown, ... (Sillebrawn, Luther)
Simpson, ... (Simpson, James)
Sisson, Giles (Sisson, Giles)
Sisson, John (not in Fed. Census)
Smalley, Elijah (Smalley, Elijah)
Smith, Asa (Smith, Asa)
Smith, Ephraim (Smith, Ephraim)
Smith, Gideon (Smith, Gideon)
Smith, Jeremiah (Smith, Jeremiah)
Smith, John (Smith, John)
Smith, ... (Smith, John)
Smith, ... (Smith, John)
Smith, Joshua (Smith, Joshua)
Smith, Samuel (Smith, Samuel)
Smith, ... (Smith, Thomas)
Smith, ... (Smith, Willm)
Smith, William (Smith, Willm)
Snyder, ... (Snider, John)
Solsbury, Job (Salisberry, Job)
Spencer, Randol (Spencer, Randall)
Spink, ... (Spink, Shibnah)
Spink, ..., Junr (Spink, Shibnah, Ju^r)
Sprague, ... (Sprague, John)
Spring, (Nath)aniel (Spring, Nathl)
Stevens, Abel (Stevens, Abel)
Stevens, Ebenezer (Stevens, Ebenezer)
Stevens, John (Stevens, John)
(S)teward, ... (Stewart, Willm)
Stewart, Elisha (Stewart, Elisha)
Stewert, Mathew (Stewart, Mathias)
Stillwill, ... (Stillvell, Barnet)

Streight, Job (Stright, Job)
Suard, Lemuel (Stewart, Lemuel)
Sutley, Gad (Suttey, Gad)
Swan, Adin (Swan, Aden)
Sweet, Amos (Sweet, Amos)
Sweet, Amos, J^r (Sweet, Amos, Ju^r)
Sweet, ... (Sweet, Asa)
Sweet, son of Caleb (Sweet, Caleb)
Sweet, Elnathan (Sweet, Elnathan)
Sweet, Isaac (Sweet, Isaac)
Sweet, Isaiah (Sweet, Isaiah)
Sweet, Jonathan (Sweet, Jonathan)
Sweet, Reuben (Sweet, Ruben)
Sweet, ... (Sweet, Silvester)
Sweet, Thomas (Sweet, Thomas)
Sweet, Thomas, J^r (Sweet, Thomas, Ju^r)
Sweet, William (Sweet, Willm)
Taber, Record (Tabor, Record)
Tannen, Abel (Tanner, Abel)
Tanner, Nathan (Tanner, Nathan)
Tanner, ... (Tanner, Palmer)
Tanner, ... (Tanner, Willm)
Taplin, Isaac (Tepland, Isaac)
Tarbox, ... (Tarbon, Jonathan)
Taylor, Jeremiah (Taylor, Jeremiah)
Taylor, John (Taylor, John)
Taylor, John, Junr (Taylor, John, Ju^r)
Taylor, Obadiah (Taylor, Obadiah)
Therben, ... (Thurber, Richard)
Thomas, Ezekiah (Thomas, Ezekiel)
Thomas, Peleg (Thomas, Peleg)
Thomas, ... (Thomas, Peleg, 3^d)
Thompson, ... (Thompson, Daniel)
Thompson, (E)lijah (Thompson, Elijah)
Thompson, Ezree (Thompson, Ezra)
Thornton, Nehemiah (Thornton, Nehemiah)
(Th)urber, ... (Thurber, Benjn)
Tiffany, Ezra (Tiffany, Ezra)
Tifft, George (Tift, George)
Tifft, James (Tift, James)
Tifft, Rufus (Tift, Rufus)
Tisdale, Samuel (Tisdale, Samuel)
Tisdale, William (Tisdale, Willm)
Townsand, James (Townsend, James)
Townsand, William (Townsend, Willm)
Trip, Job (Trip, Job)
Trumbell, Elijah (Trimble, Elijah)
Trumbell, ... (Trimble, Oliver)
Turner, (W)illiam (Turner, Willm)
(Tu)ttle, ... (Tuttle, Ared)
(T)uttle, ... (Tuttle, Willm)
Udall, John (Udall, John)
Udall, Oliver (Udall, Oliver)
Vary, ..., J^r (Varcy, Samuel, J^r)

Vaughn, ... (Vaughan, Robert)
Vaugn, ... (Vaughan, Jabez)
Vinscent, John E. (Vincent, John E.)
Vinsent, ... (Vincent, Caleb)
Vinsent, (Nic)holas (Vincent, Nicholas)
Vinson, ... (Vincent, Benjn)
Vinson, ... (Vincent, Nicholas)
Vores, William (Vooris, Willm)
Wadsworth, ... (Wadsworth, Joseph)
Wait, ... (Wait, Joseph)
Walker, Daniel (Walker, Daniel)
Walker, James (Walker, James)
Warden, Gelbart (Worden, Gilbert)
Warden, Mary (Worden, Mary)
Warden, Walter (Worden, Walter)
Warner, Benjamin (Warren, Benjn)
Warner, Benjamin, Junr (Warren, Benjn, Ju^r)
Warner, David (Warner, David)
Warrin, ... (Warren, David)
Wasson, John (Wasen, John)
Waterbury, David (Waterberry, David)
Waterbury, David, Junr (Waterberry, David, Ju^r)
Waterbury, Enos (Waterberry, Enos)
Waterman, Elisha (Waterman, Elisha)
Waterman, ... (Waterman, Samuel)
Watson, I(c)habud (Watson, Ichabod)
Watson, ... (Watson, John)
Watterman, ... (Waterman, Oliver)
Watts, Isaac (Watts, Isaac)
Weaver, ... (Weaver, Harris)
Weaver, John (Weaver, John)
Weaver, ... (Weaver, Willm)
Webster, Constant (Webster, Constant)
Wedge, Mary (Wedge, Mary)
Wells, ... (Wells, Peter)
West, James (West, James)
Westcot, Arnold (Westcoot, Arnold)
Westcot, Joseph (Westcoot, Joseph)
Westgate, James (Westcoot, James)
Whayle, Charles (Whelery, Charles)
Whaly, Thomas (Wheley, Thomas)
Wheeler, ... (Wheeler, Ezra)
Wheler, ... (Wheeler, Peter)
Whiple, Ebenezer (Whipple, Ebenezer)
Whiple, ... (Whipple, Nathan)
White, ... (White, Ichabod)
Whitebord, ... (Whitford, Christopher)
Whitford, Joshua (Whitford, Joshua)
Whitford, Joshua, Junr (Whitford, Joshua, Ju^r)
Whitteker, ... (Whittekar, Willm)
Whitter, ...h (Whittaker, Zacheus)
Wilcox, ... (Wilcox, Benjn)
Willcox, ... (Wilcox, Bridget)
Willcox, ... (Wilcox, Caleb)

Willcox, ... (Wilcox, Consider)
Willcox, John (Wilcox, John)
Willcox, ... (Wilcox, Major)
Williams, ... (Williams, Jonathan)
Williamson, Mikel (Williamson, Michael)
Winsten, ... (Winston, Abraham)
Winston, ..., Junr (Winston, Abraham, J^r)
Winston, ... (Winston, Isaac)
Winston, Jacob (Winston, Jacob)
Wiser, James (Wyers, James)
Withams, Jacob (Williams, Jacob)
Wood, ... (Wood, Silas)
Woolcutt, ... (Woolcott, Justus)
Worden, Arnold (Worden, Arnold)
Worden, Dudley (Worden, Dudley)
Worden, ... (Worden, Jesse)
Worder, William (Worden, William)
Wyburn, Isaac (Weyburn, Isaac)
Wylie, James (Wylie, James)
Wylie, John (Wylie, John)
Young, Thomas (Young, Thomas)

STILLWATER
Adams, Abijah (Adams, Abijah)
Allcock, Asa (Alcock, Asa)
Anderson, William (Anderson, Willm)
Andrews, (Delive)rance (Andrews, Deliverance)
Andrews, Ephraim (Andrews, Ephraim)
Andrews, Samuel (Andrews, Samuel)
Andrus, Elisha (Andrews, Elisha)
Andrus, Stephen (Andrews, Stephen)
Andrus, Titus (Andrews, Titus)
Armstrong, Thomas (Armstrong, Thomas)
Arnold, Thomas (Arnold, Thomas)
Baker, Amos (Baker, Amos)
Baker, Edy (Baker, Edy)
Baley, Charles (Relley, Charles)
Barber, ... (Barber, Joshua)
Bassett, Jotham (Bassett, Jotham)
Bedwell, Abraham (Bidwell, Abraham)
Bell, Henry (Bell, Henry)
Benedict, Gilbert (Benedict, Gilbert)
Benjamin, Josiah (Benjamin, Josiah)
Benjamin, Josiah, Junr (Benjamin, Josiah, J^r)
Benjamin, ... (Benjamin, Ruth)
Bennet, Jethro (Bennet, Jethro)
Berry, John (Berry, John)
Bevens, Ebner (Bevins, Abner)
Bidwell, David, Senr (Bidwell, David)
Bidwell, Jacob (Bidwell, Jacob)
Blacklee, Clement (Blackslea, Clement)
Bowler, Simeon, Senr (Baler, Simeon)
Bowler, Simeon, Junr (Baler, Simeon, Ju^r)
Brown, Calvin (Brown, Calvin)

Brown, James (Brown, James)
Burlingmore, (Heze)kiah (Burlingham, Hezekiah)
Burlingmore, ... (Burlingham, Silas)
Campbell, Solomon (Campbell, Solomon)
Carty, John (Carthy, John)
Case, James (Case, James)
Chapman, Noah (Chapman, Noah)
Chase, Joseph (Chase, Joseph)
Clapp, (Na)thaniel (Clap, Nath[l])
Clements, P(e)ter (Clements, Peter)
Concklin, Isaac (Conklin, Isaac)
Cooper, Samuel (Cooper, Samuel)
Cooper, William (Cooper, Will[m])
Corps, Joseph (Corpos, Joseph)
Corps, Nathaniel (Corps, Nath[l])
Cotter, Alexander (Cotter, Alexander)
Crosby, Timothy (Crosby, Timothy)
Demond, Charles (Dimond, Charles)
Dickenson, Daniel (Dickison, Daniel)
Dickenson, Isaac (Dickison, Isaac)
Duning, (Lew)is (Dunning, Lewis)
Duning, ... (Duning, Will[m])
Eaton, Elpheus (Eaton, Alpheus)
Embree, Rowlen (Embree, Rowland)
Ensign, Ezekiel (Ensign, Ezekiel)
Fellows, John (Fellows, John)
Finch, Ebenezer (Finch, Ebenezer)
Fish, Job (Fish, Job)
Ford, Timothy (Ford, Timothy)
Ford, William (Ford, Will[m])
Foster, Isaac (Foster, Isaac)
Foster, Vincent (Foster, Vincent)
Fullerton, Grace (Fullerton, Grant)
Gage, Jesse (Gage, Jesse)
Gauslin, John (Goslin, John)
Gilman, Daniel (Gilman, Daniel)
Gleason, William T. (Gleeson, Will[m] T.)
Gould, Jesse (Gould, Jesse)
Gould, John (Gould, John)
Green, James (Green, James)
Green, William (Green, Will[m])
Griffen, John (Griffin, John)
Hall, Simon (Hall, Simon)
Halstead, Ezekiel (Halsted, Ezekiel)
Hamblin, ... (Hamlin, Amos)
Handa, Zebulon (Handy, Zebulon)
Hawkins, Edward (Hawkins, Edward)
Heart, Jeremiah (Heart, Jeremiah)
Henderson, James (Henderson, James)
Hewett, Asa (Hewitt, Asa)
Hewett, Nathaniel (Hewitt, Nath[l])
Hewett, (Phil)ander (Hewett, Philander)
Highsted, ... (Highsted, Thaddeus)
Hodijman, Amos (Hodgeman, Amos)

Holmes, Yhomas (Holmes, Thomas)
Hopkins, Ebenezer (Hackius, Ebenezer)
Horskins, Daniel (Hoskins, Daniel)
Hunnewell, Isaiah (Honeywell, Isaiah)
Hunter, George (Hunter, George)
Hunter, ... (Hunter, John)
Hunter, Robert (Hunter, Robert)
Ingersol, Daniel (Ingersoll, Daniel)
Ireland, Stephen (Freland, Stephen)
Jackways, Phineas (Jaquish, Phineas)
Jacobs, Jonathan (Jacobs, Jonathan)
Kanor, ... (Connor, Alexander)
Keeler, Gutrich (Keeler, Gutridge)
Ketchum, Joel (Ketchem, Joel)
Lamphear, ... (Lamphear, Levi)
Lane, William (Lane, Willm)
Leet, Luther (Leet, Luther)
Leggett, Benjamin (Leggit, Benjn)
Leggett, Gabriel (Leggit, Gabriel)
Leggett, Isaac (Leggit, Isaac)
Levens, Samuel (Levins, Samuel)
Loak, Thomas (Look, Thomas)
Loveless, Joshua (Loveless, Joshua)
McBride, John (McBride, John)
McBride, Margaret (McBride, Margaret)
McCray, Alexander (McCreary, Alexander)
McCray, Samuel (McCreary, Samuel)
Mead, Noah (Mead, Noah)
Mead, William (Mead, Willm)
Merrel, Noah (Murrel, Noah)
Merrill, Elias (Merrill, Elias)
Miller, John (Miller, John)
Montgomirie, William (Montgomery, Willm)
Montgomery, Elijah (Montgomery, Elijah)
Moore, Reuben (Moore, Ruben)
More, Amos (Moore, Amos)
More, Casper (Moore, Jasper)
More, Phineas (Moore, Phineas)
Morey, ... (Moorey, Thomas)
Morrison, James (Morrison, James)
Morrison, Thomas (Morrison, Thomas)
Mott, Zebulon (Mott, Zebulon)
Mulikan, Amos (Mulligan, Amos)
Munger, Philip (Munger, Philip)
Munger, Samuel (Munger, Samuel)
Munger, Timothy (Munger, Timothy)
Nelson, Moses (Nelson, Moses)
Newland, Joseph (Newland, Joseph)
Norton, Daniel (Norton, Daniel)
Olmstead, Lemuel (Olmsted, Lemuel)
Palmer, Elias (Palmer, Elias)
Palmer, George (Palmer, George)
Palmer, Joseph (Palmer, Joseph)
Parks, Jehiel (Parks, Jehiel)

Parks, Joel (Parks, Joel)
Patrick, Ebenezer (Patrick, Ebenezer)
Patrick, ..., Junr (Patrick, Ebenezer, J^{r})
(Patric)k, ..., Junr (Patrick, Robert, Ju^{r})
(Pa)trick, ..., 2^{d} (Patrick, Robert, 2^{d})
Patrick, William (Patrick, Willm)
Peckham, Jonathan (Packham, Jonathan)
Peekham, Silas (Peckham, Silas)
Potter, Edward (Potter, Edward)
Powers, Lemuel (Powers, Lemuel)
Preston, William (Preston, Willm)
Prime, Amos (Prince, Amos)
Ram, Crisp (Kann, Cresp)
Rathboon, Benjamin (Rathbon, Benjn)
Reed, William (Reed, Willm)
Rockwell, ... (Rockwell, Simeon)
Rodes, William (Rhodes, Willm)
Rogers, Samuel (Rogers, Samuel)
Rowlie, John (Rowlie, John)
Sayler, Ahab (Sayles, Ahab)
Schuyler, Harmanus (Schuyler, Hermanus)
Schuyler, John H. (Schuyler, John H.)
Sebring, Leffert (Seabring, Leffert)
Secory, Andrew (Secor, Andrew)
Shaft, Henry (Shaft, Henry)
Shaulding, Joseph (Spalding, Joseph)
Sherman, Briggs (Sherman, Brigs)
Silliman, ... (Silliman, John)
Smith, ... (Smith, John)
Smith, William S. (Smith, Willm M.)
Stafford, Samuel (Stafford, Samuel)
Starbuck, James (Starbuck, James)
Stevens, Joseph (Stevens, Joseph)
Stevens, ... (Stevens, Phineas)
Stevens, Samuel (Stevens, Samuel)
Stewart, John (Stewart, John)
Stone, Eli (Stone, Eli)
Strahan, John (Stratron, John)
Strong, ... (Strong, Gabriel)
Swart, Dirck (Swart, Dirck)
(Swee)tland, ... (Sweetland, Willm)
Talman, David (Tolman, David)
Taylor, Israel (Taylor, Israel)
Taylor, Lemuel (Taylor, Lemuel)
Thompson, Daniel (Thompson, Daniel)
Thurber, Richard (Thurber, Richard)
Timothy (a Negro) (Tina, a Black)
Toms, Robert (Toms, Robert)
Trus, John (Ives, John)
Turner, ... (Turner, Hezekiah)
Vernor, ... (Vernor, James)
Vernor, ... (Vernor, John)
Waring, Nathaniel (Waring, Nathl)
Waters, John (Waters, John)

Watson, Cyprian (Watson, Cyprian)
Welch, Aaron (Welsh, Aaron)
Welch, David (Welsh, David)
Welch, Ebenezer (Welsh, Ebenezer)
West, Fones (West, Fones)
West, Francis (West, Francis)
West, Thomas (West, Thomas)
Weston, Lettes (Weston, Lettis)
White, Stephen (Whitehead, Stephen)
Whitford, Foster (Whitford, Foster
Whiting, (Jere)miah (Whiting, Jeremiah)
Wibert, Sarah (Wibert, Sarah)
Wilcox, Abraham (Wilcox, Abraham)
Wilcox, Roger (Wilcox, Roger)
Wilkenson, (Sam)uel (Wilkison, Samuel)
Willard, Elias (Willard, Elias)
Williams, Lewis Senr (Williams, Lewis)
Wood, John (not in Fed. Census)
Wood, Timothy (Wood, Timothy)
Woodworth, Ephraim, Seen^r (Woodworth, Ephraim)
Woodworth, Ephraim, Junr (Woodworth, Ephraim, Ju^r)
Woodworth, Reuben (Woodworth, Ruben)
Wright, Reuben (Wright, Ruben)

WATERVLIET
Abbatt, William (Abbot, William)
Able, Andries (Able, Andrew)
Abraham, Christian (Abraham, Christian)
Alexander, ... (Alexander, Hugh)
Allen, (Wil)liam (Allen, William)
Anthony, John (Anthony, John)
Ash, John (Ash, John)
Backer, Aren (Becker, Aaron)
Backer, Dirck (Becker, Direck)
Backer, Walter (Bicker, Walter)
Badgley, Anthony (Badgley, Anthony)
Baker, Benjamin (Baker, Benjamin)
Bargardus, ... P. (Bogardus, Ephraim P.)
Bartle, Elizabeth (Burtle, Elizabeth)
Bartley, Abraham (Bartley, Abraham)
Bassett, Michel (Basset, Michael)
Beard, Francis (Beard, Francis)
Bell, Stephen (Bell, Stephen)
Benedick, Stephen (Benedict, Stephen)
Bever, Thomas (Beaver, Thomas)
Bignel, Gafit (Bignel, Japhat)
Blain, Peter (Blain, Peter)
Blessing, ... (Blessing, Frederick)
Blodget, John (Blodget, John)
Bogert, Christopher (Bogert, Christopher)
Bogert, Peter (Bogert, Peter)
Boswyck, William (Bostwick, William)
Bovie, Math^s (Bovee, Matthew)
Bradt, ...

Bradt, Garret (Bradt, Garret)
Bradt, John B. (Bradt, John B.)
Brat, ... (Bradt, Albert)
Brat, William (Bradt, William)
Bratt, Christian (not in Fed. Census)
Bratt, David (Bradt, David)
Bratt, (Jac)ob (Bratt, Jacob)
Bratt, John (Bradt, John)
Bratt, John S. (Bradt, John S.)
Bratt, Storm A. (Bradt, Storm A.)
Britt, Fredrick (Britt, Frederick)
Brooks, Peter (Brooks, Peter)
Brown, George (Brown, George)
Brown, Stephen (Brown, Stephen)
Bruce, ... (Bruce, Michael)
Buel, Christof (Bewel, Christopher)
Bulsing, Benjamin (Bulsing, Benjamin)
Bulsing, Solomon (Bulsing, Solomon)
Burnside, John (Burnside, John)
Burnside, Thomas (Burnside, Thomas)
Burnside, William (Burnside, William)
Caporan, Oliver (Capron, Oliver)
Cator, Wilhelmus (Cator, Wilhelmus)
Clark, John (Clark, John)
Clark, Nathanel (Clark, Nathaniel)
Clark, Rachel (Clark, Rachel)
Clau, Lowrance (Clan, Lawrance)
Clerk, Walter (Clerk, Walter)
Clinton, Joseph (Clinton, Joseph)
Clute, Abraham (Clute, Abraham)
Clute, Nicholas (Clute, Nicholas)
Collier, George (not in Fed. Census)
Commins, Daniel (Cummings, Daniel)
Conner, ... (Conner, Edward)
Connon, Andrew (Conner, Andrew)
Coofort, ... (not in Fed. Census)
Coofort, Stephen (not in Fed. Census)
Coon, Conrath (Coon, Conradt)
Coonly, ...
Coonley, Solomon (Coonly, Solomon)
Cooper, Jacob (Cooper, Jacob)
Cooper, Obadia (Cooper, Obediah)
Cooper, Thomas (Cooper, Thomas)
Crannell, (Willi)am W. (Crannell, William Winslow)
Cregier, Bastian (Kregier, Bastian)
Cregier, Hester (Kregier, Hester)
Cregier, Martinus (Kregier, Martinus)
Crounce, Philip (Grounce, Philip)
Culings, James (Cullings, James)
Cury, Lamuel (Cary, Samuel)
Cutler, John (Cutler, John)
Deforeest, Jesse (De Freest, Jessee)
Degroat, Peter (Groat, Peter D.)
De Lamp, Tys (De Camp, Titus)

Delong, David (Delong, David)
Denbar, Levinus (Dunbar, Levinus)
Denniston, James (Davison, James)
Dents, John (Dentz, John)
Dodge, Edmond (Dodge, Edmund)
Dodge, Hezekiah (Dodge, Hezekiah)
Dods, John (Dodds, John)
Dogg, Peter (Doeg, Peter)
Dorman, Jerimiah (Dorman, Jeremiah)
Dox, (Pe)ter (Dox, Peter)
Dugles, Wieler (Douglass, Weeter)
Dump, ...ck (Damp, Frederick)
Duvepack, John (Duvepack, John)
Egberts, Anthony (Egberts, Anthony)
Enger, James (Angers, James)
Erwin, John (Irwin, John)
Farely, Joseph (Fairlie, Joseph)
Fegeler, Cosper (Feagler, Casper)
Ferguson, (Dun)can (Ferguson, David)
Ferguson, ... (Ferguson, George)
Finehout, Peter (Finehout, Peter)
Fisher, John (Visscher, John)
Flansburgh, ...
Flansburg, Daniel (Flansburgh, Daniel)
Flansburg, David (Flansburgh, David)
Flansburgh, William (Flansburgh, William)
Flare, Joseph (not in Fed. Census)
Fleeman, Andries (not in Fed. Census)
Flinn, John (Flinn, John)
Fonda, Abraham (Fonda, Abraham)
Fonda, Jacob (Fonda, Jacob)
Food, James (Foot, James)
Fort, Anjr (Fort, Anocha)
Fort, Nicholas (Fort, Nicholas)
Foulter, Francis (Fulton, Francis)
Francken, ...
Francken, ...
Fredick, Michael (Frederick, Michael)
Freeman, Silas (Freeman, Silas)
Fretts, Nicholas (Fretts, Nicholas)
Friday, Conrod (Friday, Conradt)
Fryar, John, Junr (Fryer, John, Junr)
Fryer, John (Fryer, John)
Gaffert, ... (Gifford, William)
Gardinier, ... (Gardeneer, Sarah)
Garson, Garret (Garrison, Garrit)
Gates, Stephen (Gates, Stephen)
Geralomon, Nicholas (Jeraleway, Nicholas)
Gibbery, Robert (Gibbeny, Robert)
Gibbs, William (Gibbs, William)
Gilles, John (Gillis, John)
Gold, Abil (Gold, Able)
Gonsale, Peteres (Kumsales, Petrus)
Goodfeller, Egbert (Goodfellow, Ichabod)

Griffins, William (Griffins, William)
Groat, Cornelius (Groat, Cornelius)
Groat, Dirck (Groat, Dirick)
Groesbeek, ... (Groesbeck, Gilbert)
Groesbeek, John (Groesbeck, John)
Groesbeek, Peter (Groesbeck, Peter)
Groott, [Alder]t (Groat, Aldert)
Groott, Dirck (Groat, Dirick)
Hallenbeek, Jacob (Hollenbeck, Jacob)
Hallenbeek, Michael (Hallenbeck, Michael)
Hamestreet, John (Hamestral, John)
Hank, Jacob (Houk, Jacob)
Haple, Francis (Hoppold, Francis)
Hashwill, John (Haswell, John)
Haswill, Robert (Haswell, Robert)
(Haws)berger, ... (Hawsbergen, Daniel)
Heans, George (Haynes, George)
Heemstreet, Dirck (Hemstral, Direck)
Heemstreet, Isaac (Heamstral, Isaac)
Hemilton, Jenne (Hamilton, Jane)
Henry, ...
Hert, David (Heart, David)
Heswall, Joseph (Ashwell, Joseph)
Hill, Elijah (Hill, Elijah)
Hilton, Jonathan (Hilton, Jonathan)
Hirek, Daniel (Herrick, Daniel)
Hoesfoot, ... (Horsford, Reuben)
Hogen, George (Hogan, George)
Hoghtalen, Johnnis H. (Houghtalen, John H.)
Hoghtalen, Teunes (Houghtalin, Teunis)
Hoghtalen, William (Houghtalen, William)
Houghtalen, Gerret (Houghtalen, Garret)
Hoke, Johannis (Hoke, Johannes)
Horkerel, Ryckard (not in Fed. Census)
Horn, Peter (Horn, Peter)
Hosener, Nicholas (Hosmer, Nicholas)
Houck, (Nichol)as (Houck, Nicholas)
Hudson, Moses (Hudson, Moses)
Hunderer, Samuel (Hundicker, Samuel)
Jacobs, Jacob (Jacobs, Jacob)
Jacobs, Wilson (Jacobs, Wilson)
James, Thomas (James, Thomas)
Johnson, Evert (Johnston, Evert)
Johnson, James (Johnston, James)
Johnson, John (Johnston, John)
Johnson, William (not in Fed. Census)
Johnston, Mary (Johnston, Mary)
Jolley, (Hu)gh (Jolly, Hugh)
Kranckhite, ... (Cronkite, Casper)
Kranckhite, Gilbert (Cronkite, Gilbert)
Kranckhite, Jesse (Cronkite, Jessie)
Lamfere, Nicholas (Lamberse, Nicholas)
Lane, Nathaniel (Lane, Nathaniel)
Lansing, Abraham H. (Lansing, Abraham H.)

Lansing, ... (Lansing, Garret)
Lansing, Jacob F. (Lansing, Jacob F.)
Lansing, Jacob H. (Lansing, Jacob H.)
Lansing, Levines F. (not in Fed. Census)
Larraway, ... (Larraway, Nicholas)
Larway, Jonas (Larraway, Jonas)
Legrange, Christian (Legrange, Christian)
Legrange, Christian J. (Legrange, Christian J.)
Legrange, Conradt (Legrange, Conradt)
Legrange, Isaac (Legrange, Isaac)
Legrange, Jacob, Junr (Legrange, Jacob, Junr)
Legrange, John J. (Legrange, John J.)
Legrange, Orne (Legrange, Omie S.)
Leonard, John (Leonard, John)
Leroye, (Wi)lliam (Larraway, William)
Levalley, ...eck (Lavally, Cook)
Lisswill, John (Liswell, John)
Livingston, Johannis (Livingston, Johannes)
Livingston, Peter (Livingston, Peter)
Looke, Jacob (Luke, Jacob)
Lotterege, Ann (Lutridge, Hannah)
Low, Thomas (Low, Thomas)
Lowery, James (Lowry, James)
Loxson, ... (Lexon, Class)
Lumeree, Daniel (Lummeree, Daniel)
Lumeree, James (not in Fed. Census)
Luther, John (Luther, John)
Lyker, ...ick (Lyker, Hendrick)
McCalven, Daniel (McCalvin, Daniel)
McCollock, William (McCollough, William)
McCutchen, Peter (McKutchen, illegible)
McGee, James (McGee, James)
McGee, John (McGee, John)
McGill, William (McGill, William)
McHary, Peter (McKargh, Peter)
McIntash, John (McIntosh, John)
Magreger, Malkum (McGrigger, Malcom)
Makentyh, Elexander (McIntosh, Alexander)
Man, ... (Mann, John)
Mareday, Helitie (Merridy, Hillida)
Marshell, Francis (Marshal, Francis)
Mason, James (Mason, James)
(M)atchcraft, ... (Matchcraft, John)
Melashim, David (Meachum, David)
Mills, Samuel (Mills, Samuel)
Milton, William (Milton, William)
Minkler, Esias (Minckler, Isaiah)
Moke, Francis (Moke, Francis)
Moke, John (Moke, John)
Mollen, ...
Molter, Philip (Mutter, Philip)
Monck, Christophel (Monk, Christopher)
Morkle, John (Merkle, John)
Morrell, Samuel (Morrell, Samuel)

Munshis, Thomas (Monchus, Thomas)
Murphy, ... (Murphy, Patrick)
Myers, ...m (Myers, Ephraim)
Myers, ... (Myers, Philip)
Nessel, Christeain (Nestley, Christian)
Nessel, George (Nestler, George)
Nickel, Francis (Nichols, Francis)
Noble, Heckiah (Noble, Hezekiah)
Noje, James (Noye, James)
Nortrip, Curnel (Nortrip, Cornel)
Ollever, Aron (Oliver, Arie)
Ollever, Jacobus (Oliver, Jacobus)
Ollever, John (Oliver, John)
Ollever, John, Junr (Oliver, John, Junr)
Oothout, Henry, Junr (Oothout, Hendrick)
Oothout, Volkert (Oothout, Volkert)
Ouderkerk, Andries (Onderkirk, Andrew)
Ouderkerk, Cornelius (Onderkirk, Cornelius)
Ouderkerk, John (Onderkirk, John)
Ouderkerck, John (Onderkirk, John)
Ouderkerk, Widow (Onderkirk, Magdaline)
Ouderkerbtk, Myndert (Onderkirk, Mendirt)
Ouderkerk, Peterus (Onderkirk, Petrus)
Ozbaart, ...ph (Ozbart, Joseph)
Parmer, Durias (Palmer, Darias)
Pasinger, (A)ndres (Pacinger, Andrew)
Pattison, William (Patterson, William)
Pepper, William (Pepper, William)
Perry, Obadiah (Perry, Obediah)
Person, ... (Parson, Joseph)
Philips, Joshua (Phelps, Joshua)
Pike, Samuel (Pike, Samuel)
Pinkerton, James (Pinkerton, James)
Pool, William (Pool, William)
Post, Benjamin (Post, Benjamin)
Povert, ... (Povert, Daniel)
Prise, Isaac (Price, Isaac)
Prize, Seth (Price, Seth)
Quackenbush, Adreain (Quackenbuss, Adrian)
Redeker, Peter (Rediker, Peter)
Redlif, Peter (Radliff, illegible)
Reese, George (Rees, George)
Relyea, David, Junr (Rellyea, David, Junr)
Rikeson, Abednego (Rickerson, Abednego)
Ripenbarg, Adam (Repenburgh, Adam)
Ripenbarg, Daniel (Repenburgh, Daniel)
Robertson, (An)drew (Robinson, Andrew)
Robison, (Ro)bert (Robinson, Robert)
Rouse, ... (Rousseau, Francis)
Row, Wilhelmus (Row, Wilhelmus)
Runcle, ... (Runkle, John, Junr)
Salsbury, Joseph (Salisburry, Joseph)
Schenck, Paulus (Schanck, Paul)

Schoomaker, Henry (Schonmaker, Henry)
Seger, Gerret (Segar, Garret)
Sharp, ... (Sharp, Gilbert)
Shaver, (Cha)rles (Shaver, Charles)
Shaver, John (Shaver, John)
Shears, Peter (Shave, Peter)
Sheely, John (Shuley, John)
Shell, Philip (Shell, Philip)
Shelley, ... (Shelly, William)
Sickels, (Abrah)am (Sickles, Abram)
Sickels, Lodewyck (Sickles, Lodowick)
Siemon, Isaac (Seaman, Isaac)
Sixbey, Evert (Sixby, Evert)
Sixbee, Nicholas A. (Sixby, Nicholas A.)
Sixby, Nicholas E. (Sixby, Nicholas E.)
Skinner, Solomon (Skinner, Solomon)
Slater, (Ro)bert (Slater, Robert)
(Sling)erland, ... (Slingerland, Isaac)
Slingerlant, Arent (Slingerland, Aaron)
Slingerlant, Tuenis W. (Slingerland, Tuenis W.)
Slingerlant, Wouter (Slingerland, Walter)
Smith, Andrew (Smith, Andrew)
Smith, Elias (Smith, Elias)
Smith, John (Smith, John)
Smith, John, Junr (Smith, John)
Smith, Nicholas (Smith, Nicholas)
Smith, Wilhelmus (Smith, Wilhelmus)
Soop, Conraat (Saop, Conradt)
Souls, Jonathan (Souls, Jonathan)
Spaan, Philip (Spawn, Philip)
Spaarbeck, Martines (Sparback, Martin)
Springsteen, Joseph (Springsteel, Joseph)
Staats, Barent (Staats, Barent)
Stansel, Yett (Stanson, Ejett)
Starr, Eliah (Starr, Elisha)
Stevens, John (Stevens, John)
Taylor, Lucas (Taylor, Lucas)
Ten Eyck, Andries (Ten Eyck, Andress)
Throbridg, Luther (Trowbridge, Luther)
Tilfort, ... (Tilford, Adam)
Tilman, John (Tillman, John, Junr)
Tilman, Richard (Tillman, Richard)
Tilman, William (Tillman, William)
Tolyk, Charles (Tolleker, Charles)
Tomkins, ...
Totton, Samuel (Totten, Samuel)
Truax, Isaac (Truax, Isaac)
Truax, Isaac, Junr (Truax, Isaac, Junr)
Truax, Jelles (Truax, Jellis)
Truax, Peter (Truax, Peter)
Tupper, William (Tupper, William)
Turck, Anthony (Turk, Anthony)
Turner, Peter (Turner, Peter)
Tymese, Bastian (Timissic, Bastian)

Utter, John (Utter, John)
Valck, Cornelius (not in Fed. Census)
Valck, Johanis (Volk, Johannes)
Van Allen, ... (Van Aulen, John)
Van Alstine, Abraham (Van Alstine, Abraham)
Van Antwerp, Ab^m (Van Antwerp, Abraham)
Van Arnem, Isaac (Van Arnum, Isaac)
Van Arnem, (Will)iam (Van Arnum, William)
Van Arnum, ... (Van Arnum, Jacob)
Van Auken, Petrus (Van Aukin, Petrus)
V D Bergh, Cornelius (Vandenburgh, Cornelius)
Van Den Bergh, Cornelius (Vandenburgh, Cornelius)
V D Bergh, Gerret (Van Bergh, Garret)
Van Den Bergh, Levinus (Vandenburgh, Levinus)
Van Den Berg, Wynant (Vandeburgh, Vinant)
V D Bergh, Wilhelmis (Vanderburgh, Wilhelmus)
Van Der Bergh, Abraham (Vandenburgh, Abraham)
Vanderzea, Cornelius S. (Van Der Zee, Cornelius)
Van Deshider, John (not in Fed. Census)
Van Dewaters, Cornelius (Vanderwater, Cornelius)
Van Kamp, Teunis (Van Camp, Teunis)
Van Loon, Joohn (in Freehold in Fed. Census)
Van Olenda, Petrus (Van Olinda, Peter)
Van Plank, David (Verplank. David)
Van Santvoort, Anthony (Vansandford, Anthony)
Van Schaick, Egbort (Van Schaick, Egbert)
Van Sent, Gilbert (Van Zant, Gilbert)
Van Sent, Joseph (Van Zant, Joseph)
Van Wagnor, Barent (Van Waggoner, Barent)
Van Wee, Abigal (Van Wee, Abigail)
Van Wee, Henry H. (Van Wee, Henry H.)
Van Wie, Hendrick (Van Wee, Hendrick)
Veeder, Lucas W. (Veeder, Lucas W.)
Verplank, John (Verplank, John)
Vieley, Jacob (there is a Jacob in Schaghticoke)
Vine, John (Vine, John)
Visscher, ... (Visscher, Bastian F.)
Volk, Matius (Volk, Matthias)
Vosburgh, (Abra)ham (Vossburgh, Abraham)
Vosburgh, Gerret (Vossburgh, Garrit)
Vosburgh, Isaac (Vossbergh, Isaac)
Vosburgh, John (Vossburgh, John)
Vrancken, ...
Vredenburg, the Widow (Vreedenburgh, Alida)
Vrooman, ...
Vrooman, Walter (Vrooman, Walter)
Waggoner, John (Waggoner, John)
Wagnor, George (Waggoner, George)
Waldron, Cornelius (Waldron, Cornelius)
Walls, John (Walts, John)
Wandell, Philip (Wendell, Philip)
Ward, Ebenezer (Ward, Ebenezer)
Watson, James (Watson, James)
Weaver, Johannis, Junr (Weaver, Johannes, Junr)

Weaver, ... [Weaver, Volintine]
Weight, Joseph [Weight, Joseph]
Wells, Henry [Wells, Henry]
Wells, Tunes [Wells, Teunis]
Wendell, ... [Wendell, Hendrick]
Wineboap, Evert [Wynkoop, Evert]
Winne, Adam [Winny, Adam]
Winne, Anthony [Winne, Anthony]
Winne, [Cor]nelius [Winney, Cornelius]
Winne, Daniel [Winney, Daniel]
Winne, David F. [Winney, David F.]
Winne, Francis [Winney, Francis]
Winne, Jan [Winney, John]
Winne, [Pe]ter F. [Winney, Peter F.]
Winne, William [Winney, William]
Winter, Michel [Winter, Michael]
Witbeek, John J. [Witbeck, John J.]
Witbeek, Woulter [Witbeck, Walter]
Wittiker, Gertreu [Witaker, Gertrude]
Wolf, Johannis [Wolf, John]
Wood, Jeremiah [Wood, Jeremiah]
Wormer, Abraham [Wormer, Abraham]
Yates, Christopher A. [Yates, Christopher A.]

www.ingramcontent.com/pod-product-compliance
Lightning Source LLC
Chambersburg PA
CBHW052106270326
41931CB00012B/2904